D1562352

THE ART OF FICTION

KAPNICK FOUNDATION
DISTINGUISHED
WRITER-IN-RESIDENCE
LECTURES FOR 2014

JAMES SALTER

The Art of Fiction

University of Virginia Press

CHARLOTTESVILLE | LONDON

University of Virginia Press
© 2016 by the James Salter Literary Trust
All rights reserved
Printed in the United States of America on acid-free paper

First published 2016

ISBN 978-0-8139-3905-6 (cloth)
ISBN 978-0-8139-3906-3 (e-book)

9 8 7 6 5 4 3 2 1

Library of Congress Cataloging-in-Publication Data
is available from the Library of Congress.

CONTENTS

INTRODUCTION

John Casey

If you haven't read any books by James Salter, should you read these lectures first? Maybe. Certainly the first one, "The Art of Fiction." You would get a sense of his voice, of his rhythm—his perfectly timed abruptnesses, which are agreeable surprises—that is, you agree to stop and let the echo clarify.

The first lecture is in the main about several great works of fiction. They are works Salter took to heart, his major allegiances. In the case of Isaac Babel, Salter mentions how he first heard of him. Salter was forty-four. "Up until the time I met Robert Phelps, everything I knew I had learned by myself. I had formed my tastes by myself, and he refined them by introducing me to new writers and resituating many of the old. I trusted him."

This is a generous acknowledgement. Salter was a generous man, but precise in his generosity. When it comes to some other authors of books on Salter's list of exemplary writers he is wittily precise. Of Hemingway Salter notes—not in the lecture—that Hemingway was "a man whose habit, both in writing and in life, was not to pass up an insult."

Salter took Phelps's recommendation of these Babel stories. "'Read this one first,' he said. It was the story called 'My First Goose.'"

Phelps was wiser than I was when I assigned to a graduate seminar all of the Red Cavalry stories and some of the drastic Odessa stories all in one week. It was too much for them—not the number of pages, but the shock of terrible violence written with terrible beauty. Salter, who had been a fighter pilot in the Korean War, "read Babel's stories again and again." He describes how Babel "is somehow able to look down on the mayhem happening all about him with the forbearance of God."

Salter was pigeonholed for some time as a "writers' writer." That *could* be a compliment. It is true that Salter has fervent admirers from the honor roll of his well-qualified literary contemporaries. But that phrase "writers' writer" isn't a blurb that attracts browsers in bookstores or online. It also has an unfortunate resonance with "gentleman's gentleman." Richard Ford, God bless him, agreed with Salter not to introduce each other to a sold-out audience at the 92nd Street Y, simply to say their own name and begin. As Salter rose to the lectern, Ford said in an audible aside to Jim, "no one is going to say 'writers' writer' anymore."

"I hope not," Salter replied.

THE Kapnick Distinguished Writer-in-Residence position was intended to reinstitute a position held by William Faulkner in the mid-1950s, an idea suggested by the endower's daughter. It occurred to me that it would also be good and compatible to use the Norton Lectures at Harvard as a model, rather than to use the appointment as an additional faculty member of our already existing Master of Fine Arts staff. Faulkner was not a faculty member, nor are the Norton lecturers. One decanal notion was that the appointment be for three to five years and that it should be awarded to a Nobel Prize winner or close to it. I made some preliminary informal inquiries. One emphatic answer was, "I don't want a *job!* But I'll be happy to consider a shorter visit, give a series of lectures. And a reading or two. And talk to students." We compiled or were given lists of prizewinners. Prize committees don't always get it right, not the Nobel, not the Booker, not the Pulitzer nor the National Book Award. Whom do we love? James Salter.

That idea got a lot of collateral support. For the first Salter lecture the hall was filled, and for the second and third lectures, standing room only. For the public reading we needed a bigger theater.

The three of us who introduced the lectures each picked a favorite Salter book of fiction. Mark Saunders, a novelist and director of the University of Virginia Press, picked *A Sport and a Pastime*, a book whose singular doubleness he delights in. Christopher Tilghman picked *Dusk*, a book he acknowledged as pivotal in his own development as a writer. I chose *Light Years*. It was the first Salter book I read, in the early 1980s, and I'd been bowled over. I was about to learn, halfway through Salter's first lecture, that it "turned out not to be a success. It was published but had a devastating, followed by a second, indifferent, review in the *Times*." Now, on page 9 of the typed-up lecture, I have added in the margin, "Until later!" It was first published in 1975 and has been in print ever since. It will be for years to come. I've reread it twice, gone back to it many more times to find favorite passages and to figure out how Salter managed to be so clear so succinctly.

I've read *A Sport and a Pastime* three times. The first time I liked it but I didn't really get it all. I was dazzled by the energy of the erotic scenes. The next time I loved it, chiefly for the ode to France, her smaller cities, towns, and countryside. It was the third time, after listening carefully to Mark Saunders over a long lunch, that the whole thing came together for me—its "singular doubleness." There is a love affair, but there is the first-person narrator who is an envious friend of the man having the affair. The narrative is imagined, imagined but eerily knowing.

Salter loved France and French literature—he is as good at explicating a crucial passage in Balzac's *Old Goriot* as Erich Auerbach is in his critical masterpiece *Mimesis. A Sport and a Pastime* is a very French novel and an American one as well. The two American men, both the lover and the imaginer, are linked to America by invisible transatlantic cables. Each has found a kind of refuge in France, but neither one is a refugee. The French woman has a link, but it is a dream: that her lover will take her to a new life in the new world. The novel was rejected. It was George Plimpton who saw what it was and arranged its publication. The coincidental catalyst was that they met in Paris.

Salter's life was full of coincidences. This is in part because he lived in many different places and was involved in various kinds of activities (West Point, the army air corps of World War II and the air force in Korea and after, literary New York, Middleburg and Upperville, Virginia, Paris, mountain climbing in the

French Alps, skiing in the Swiss Alps, moviemaking in America and Italy, a conversational evening with Nabokov in Montreux). The coincidences come in greater part because he was curious, observant, and had a prodigious memory both visual and verbal. He was also open to his friendly impulses. *Burning the Days,* his memoir, has many short paragraphs about meeting someone that end with "I liked him immediately," or "she was authentic."

MANY years ago I drove up to Washington to hear Salter lecture. Afterwards I went up to him to say how much I liked his talk and to ask him a question. He said, "Why don't you come to dinner with us?"

I read more of his books over the next decade or two.

It came time to invite our first Kapnick Distinguished Writer-in-Residence. I got his address from my agent. One of my paragraphs began, "You may not remember . . ." He wrote back saying he was interested in coming to the university, and he remembered our meeting well. "You drove us to the restaurant. You said to yourself, 'The traffic isn't fluid,' implying some time spent in Italy." Yes. My Italian friends often grumbled, "Il trafico non è fluido."

I read *Burning the Days.* On page 24: "at a luncheon, I sat next to a green-eyed young woman, a poet, who declared loftily that you learned nothing from books, it was life you learned from, passion, experience. The host, a fine old man in his seventies, heard her and disagreed. His hair was white. His voice had the faint shrillness of age. 'No, everything I've ever learned,' he said, 'has come from books. I'd be in darkness without them.'"

I had heard that fine old man's voice with the "faint shrillness of age." I knew how he read. It sounded like Uncle Courty, my favorite uncle-in-law.

I stopped reading and sent Salter a note quoting the passage that had stopped me. I added "Courty Barnes?" The reply: "Yes. I liked him. I liked him even more for what he said."

All this would have been confirmed had I read the next paragraph:

"I didn't know if he was speaking of Balzac or Strindberg or even John O'Hara, to whom his sister had been married."

It was a novelistic pleasure to find myself caught on an outer strand of James Salter's web of coincidences. It was, more important, a bond. I had loved Courty Barnes. A shared friendship is a good start. Shared books. In Charlottesville, where Salter took up his Kapnick residency in 2014, my wife and I were blessed with an Indian summer and a fall full of congenial companionship with him and Kay, on our back porch or in the house he and Kay rented.

Jim told stories very well. Easily and succinctly. His own stories and ones he'd heard or read. His own voice not shrilled by age but softened. A story from *Out of Africa*, Isak Dinesen and the French sommelier. The sommelier is intent on hiking into the bush, a suicidal notion. He stops at Isak Dinesen's house to say goodbye. She brings out her best bottle of wine. An almost whispered punch line, the word the Frenchman says after his first sip, *"Fameux."* It is the second meaning of *"fameux"*: first rate, magnificent.

When I gave Jim a book of my own essays on the art of fiction, I mentioned that one of them dealt with how to keep two narrative lines going simultaneously.

"Oh?"

"I found four good examples. In Nabokov, Flaubert, Chekhov, and Salter."

"What are those other guys doing in there?"

For some reason that reminded me of remarks Jim remembered and recorded from his days in Korea. MIGs appear behind two US planes.

Wingman to leader: "Lead, they're shooting at us!"

Lead: "That's OK, they're allowed to do that."

Aplomb is something Jim admires. One of the many things.

IT IS sometimes disconcerting to read a fiction writer's memoir. It can become dense with names. I also found that I didn't want to know the factual origins of the story, at least not before reading the story.

In *Burning the Days* there are a couple of anecdotes that later become full art, but most sections are as taut as Salter's fiction. The straightforward autobiography in the parts about West Point, about learning to fly and to fly in combat, are riveting. *The Hunters,* Salter's first novel, about the air war over the Yalu River, is very good, but eclipsed by the seventy pages in *Burning the Days* of what it was like for him in full first person. The pages begin: "Late in the summer of 1951 I entered at last the realm long sought and was sent to Presque Isle, Maine, to the 75th fighter squadron. . . . I felt I was born for it." These pages end with, "Once at a dinner party I was asked by a woman what on earth I had ever seen in military life. I couldn't answer her, of course." But then with memory and reflection, he tells us.

Another theme: friendship. Salter loved Irwin Shaw. The chapter title is "Forgotten Kings." Shaw's books were widely read fifty or sixty years ago. I remember my parents and uncles and aunts talking about them. Shaw was on top. In Hemingway's eyes Shaw was a rival, perhaps as much for manliness as for literary reputation.

Shaw took up Salter. Their second meeting was for lunch at Shaw's Paris apartment. Lunch for three: Shaw, his wife, Marian, and Salter. "There was the ease and implication of French life, unseen gatherings all about us. . . . It was the end of the fifties, the years of the Sulzbergers, the Matthiessens, Plimpton, Teddy White. A family lunch, and I was already seeing him as a kind of father—my own was gone—a father like Dumas or an ex-boxing champion, something in him extravagant, never to be taken away."

Salter pays many tributes to the man, remembers his generosity, the size of his life. There are also examples of Shaw losing his temper; Shaw once hit a man who said to him repeatedly, "You're a good writer, why are you such a whore?"

Or a cruel remark. "'Well, I've done it again,' a writer who'd had great early success remarked to him. 'Don't say that,' Irwin said. 'You didn't do it the first time.'"

About a film Salter made of a story by Shaw, Shaw said that Salter was a lyric and Shaw a narrative writer. "'Lyric' seemed a word he was uncomfortable with. It seemed to mean something like callow."

The end of the chapter is on the end of Irwin Shaw's life. Salter grieves for him. The last three pages are heartfelt, painful elegy. Of a visit to Shaw near the end: "He lay in bed thinking, like a blind sailor remembering the sea."

SALTER ended up with a low opinion of the movie business. That part of *Burning the Days* is hectic with meetings, most of which are inconsequential except for memorable names (Maximilian Schell, Maggie Smith, Vanessa Redgrave, Roman Polanski). He likes them and admires them. They stand out from those scurrying and jostling, even those scurriers and jostlers who achieve meteoric success. "I've always rejected the idea of actor as hero, and no intimacy has changed that. Actors are idols. Heroes are those with something at stake."

Salter did have a genuine liking for Robert Redford, with whom he made a good movie, *Downhill Racer.* Salter admired the way that Redford did something useful every day. He liked Redford because he was down-to-earth, loved nature, and did all he could to help preserve the environment. And later, Jim immensely admired Redford's use of his reputation and clout to establish Sundance, which Jim considered a real and ongoing contribution to film.

The movie section of *Burning the Days* is a cautionary tale—something to pass along to a niece or a nephew whose eyes have stardust in them. Salter got *something* out of it, but it took a lot out of him.

In these lectures Jim doesn't discuss his short stories as he does his novels, even when he's selling a couple of his novels short. *The Hunters* is one he thought I could skip. He was wrong; it's very well made and has a lot of the ecstasy—ecstasy is what Jim wanted to be the core of his writing—that shows up in the section on flying in the memoir *Burning the Days*. Certainly flying combat missions in Korea. But always the amazement of being airborne. To be Icarus and live.

I think flying was a foundational experience for Jim. That he was as amazed by great literature as by flying is a measure of his mind. That he resigned from the air force and chose to write fiction is a measure of his allegiance to that second amazement.

In flying, an essential sense is sight, and Jim's short stories depend on sight. In this he is like Joseph Conrad, who wrote about his own work, "Above all, I want to make you see." To urge you to read *Dusk* the way Robert Phelps urged Jim to read Isaac Babel's stories by naming three, I'd pick "Dirt," "The Destruction of the Goetheanum," and "The Cinema."

"Dirt" is a simple story. A very old man is building a new foundation for an old house. "Death was coming for Harry Mies. He would lie emptied, his cheeks rouged, the fine, old man's ears unhearing. There was no telling the things he knew. He was alone in the far fields of his life." Future conditional, blink, back to present.

Harry has a young man helping him to raise the floor so they can pour a concrete base.

> "Feller could start right there," Harry called.
> "This one?"
> "That's it."
> Billy slowly wiped the dirt from his eyes again and began to set up the jack. The joists were a few inches above his face.

They are in the heat of the American Southwest. No state named, could be a flat piece of Arizona or New Mexico. Or Colorado a good way before it lifts. The only bar in town is full of ranch hands. Harry never goes in. Billy does. The ranch hands notice him only to talk about him. Billy is seeing the only girl in town. The ranch hands keep track of him through the front window.

> "That's Billy."
> "Yeah, that's him."

"Well, what do you think?" They laid out phrases in low voices, like bets. Their arms were big as firewood on the bar. "Is he going to it or coming from it?"

Harry and Billy are close in their work. The old man mixes the first barrow load of concrete. "On the second trip he let Billy push the barrow, naked to the waist, the sun roaring down on his shoulders and back, his muscles jumping as he lifted. The next day he let him shovel."

A few words. Exact instances of labor. The sun. But the lasting impression is of something else. In his second lecture Jim says, "Writers have an affinity with painters. . . . With landscape, of course, there is the absolute, unalterable depiction of a real place. . . . The backgrounds, too, when you look at them, are instructive, sometimes remarkably plain. You didn't notice it because the picture was made so that your attention never went to the background. It was carried off without your even noticing."

In a way "Dirt" is about constricted lives, some bitter, two with the relief of being shared. But: "With landscape, of course, there is the absolute, unalterable depiction of a real place." There are sun and dust, but also an implicit vast Southwest.

Harry has died. "He looked like a pharaoh there in the funeral home." Billy and Alma leave in a car they bought for a hundred dollars. "The sun polished the windshield . . . going southward."

For all that is explicitly visible, there is the implicitly visible landscape. The sense of that is essential.

PETER Taylor occasionally taught a fiction writing class at Harvard. He didn't insist but clearly preferred that the students write short stories. Someone asked him, "What is a short story?"

Peter said, "A one-act play."

The next week he said, "A short story is like a poem, but without the display." Peter knew poets. His old friend Robert Lowell, Randall Jarrell, his brother-in-law Donald Justice. Peter's wife, Eleanor Ross Taylor, was a very good poet. Peter may have just been making some breathing room for his preferred genre.

The third week Peter said, "The short story does the work of a novel in fifteen pages."

"THE Destruction of the Goetheanum" is fifteen pages. The first sentence: "In the garden, standing alone, he found the young woman who was the friend of the writer William Hedges, then unknown but even Kafka had lived in obscurity, she said, and so moreover had Mendel, perhaps she meant Mendeleyev."

The first sentence contains all of the elements of the story but the grandest. He is *he*. The young woman is called Nadine. "'I was born in Genoa,' she told him." It seems for a while that the story is to be a triangle, that most basic of forms of plane geometry.

Hedges is writing a novel. "'It's called *The Goetheanum,*' she said. 'Do you know what that is?'"

The Goetheanum was in the first place a monument to Goethe. It was built in Dornach, Switzerland, not far from Basel, completed during the First World War. It was designed by Rudolf Steiner to honor Goethe, but also to be the center of a community of followers of Steiner.

"'Who is Steiner?' he asked."

She explains. What she relates is factual: what Steiner believed in, what he taught, and that he had many followers. "And somehow from this she had learned a scenario. She had become the illusionist of Hedges' life."

The building is the most certain element in the story: "Two enormous domes which intersected, the plot of that curve itself was a mathematical event. . . . Small, tributary domes like helmets contained the windows and doors. . . . The construction was carried on by people from all over the world, many of them abandoned professions and careers."

The three characters, their not so predictable wanderings towards each other, away from each other, almost don't matter. One feels a puzzled sympathy. It is the last page about the building that arouses pity and terror. It is also as beautiful as a Turner painting.

IN "The Cinema," there is a cast of characters of interest. There are many others popping in and out. They are making a movie in Rome. There is a beautiful leading lady; a past-his-prime leading man; the dircctor; the producer; the publicity girl (*sic*), Eva. This list is in order of appearance, not importance, at least not in the hierarchy of moviemaking.

We never know nor do we need to know the plot of the film. It is the harum-scarum day-and-night life of the production—the alliances, the backbiting, the egos, the falterings—that is in the spotlight. Each of the six characters of interest takes a turn or two.

The scriptwriter is smitten with the leading lady. Old Hollywood joke: The aspiring actress who was so clueless she slept with the writer. The leading lady is not that clueless, but she lives in a haze of her own beauty. The leading man says a dazzlingly stupid thing about women's intelligence: "'A woman's whole essence is here. . . . The womb. . . . Nowhere else. Do you realize there are no great women bridge players?'"

Her reaction: "She was content to be what he admired in a woman. . . . Beneath the table, her hand discovered his."

The director, Iles:

> It was now Iles' turn, the time to expose his ideas. He plunged in. He was like a kind of crazy schoolmaster as he described the work, part Freud, part lovelorn columnist. . . . Members of the crew had sneaked in to stand near the door. Guivi jotted something in his script.
>
> "Yes, notes, make notes," Iles told him. "I am saying some brilliant things."

The most understandable characters, that is, the most locatable, outside the mania, are Eva and Lang, the scriptwriter. We are given glimpses of Eva's life:

> She lived at home. Her family ate without speaking, four of them in the sadness of bourgeois surroundings. . . . When he was finished, her father cleared his throat. The meat was better the last time, he said. The *last* time? Her mother asked.
>
> "Yes, it was better," he said.

"The last time it was tasteless."

"Ah, well, two times ago," he said.

The snippet of ordinary sadness is sad of course but also a relief.

Eva and her friend Mirella, who works in publicity, discuss the stars and chiefs. Mirella: "The producer: first of all, he was impotent. When he wasn't impotent, he was unwilling, and the rest of the time he didn't know how to go about it and when he did, it was unsatisfactory." The producer has also had a go at Eva. "'I tried to pretend it was all a joke.'" The omniscient narrator: "They knew everything. They were like the nurses whose tenderness was dead. It was they who ran the sick house. They knew how much money everyone was getting, who were not to be trusted."

Is it out of pity that Eva eats supper with Lang, the scriptwriter? Or is it his pity? Or both their solitudes? Everyone else has gone off to a big party. After supper Lang and Eva park outside the Botanical Gardens, the car windows are frosted.

"I am so lonely," she said suddenly. . . .
Her breath was in crystals, visible in the dark.
"Can I kiss it?" she said.
She began to moan then, as if it were holy. She

touched it with her forehead. She was murmuring. The nape of her neck was bare.

She called the next morning. It was eight o'clock.

"I want to read something to you," she said.

. . . Her voice entered his body, it commanded his blood.

Salter continues to accelerate, as if the needle in a record-player arm is now skipping more than one groove—two or more grooves. She reads aloud a brief passage from an article about a gala in Milan in 1868.

> *It was the event of the year, crowded and gay, and while the world of fashion amused itself thus, at the same hour and in the same city a lone astronomer was discovering a new planet. . . .*
> Silence. *A new planet.*

Usually toward the end of a hectic story, either the narrative slows down and becomes sonorous or it cracks a whip. I expected one or the other after Eva's nicely chosen gift. But this ending is, like the ending of the "The Destruction of the Goetheanum," terrible and beautiful. "He heard her call his name. He said nothing. He lay there becoming small, smaller, vanishing. The room became a window, a façade, a group of buildings, squares and sections, in the end all of Rome. His ecstasy was beyond knowing. The roofs of the great cathedrals shone in the winter air."

This is not so clear a final note as "Ah, Bartleby! Ah, humanity!"—but it sets off an echo of it. That is one way I have read this story. How forthright and eager Eva was to give Lang sexual pleasure. We don't know if he returned the favor. The morning after, she finds an out-of-the-way anecdote and reads it to him over the phone. It is a balm to his having been treated as . . . well, the scriptwriter. He says nothing. He is in ecstasy. His ecstasy is a vision. A cinematic dissolving that ends with a still picture of the baroque cathedrals of Rome. He sees it alone. I try to hope: is it possible that he will be loving to Eva afterwards? Or at least grateful? But then I thought of another ending, just as forlorn as "Bartleby the Scrivener," but more biting. It is what Jake says to Lady Brett when she imagines out loud that the two of them could have been happy together: "Isn't it pretty to think so?"

Salter's ending is technically and emotionally in the same league as Melville's and Hemingway's.

LAST NIGHT is Salter's other collection of stories, seven years after *Dusk*. The stories in *Last Night* have very different astonishments from those in *Dusk*. "Platinum" is a descendent of a number of well-made stories that depend on a piece of jewelry. Maupassant wrote one, as did Louise de Vilmorin, and Somerset Maugham. "Platinum" is as well made as those and to my mind has deeper dimensions.

"Arlington" is about two sorts of sadness. The first is that of an army officer, Newell, who marries a dazzling younger woman, an exotic Czech beauty. "Peter, pumpkin eater, had a wife and couldn't keep her." The other sadness is that of that officer's bungled army career. One can infer that he stole radios from supplies and sold them in order to bring Jana's parents from Czechoslovakia.

The final scene is of a burial at Arlington, the burial of the senior officer who supported Newell, his junior officer, to no avail. But the ceremony enables the court-martialed ex-officer to find a solid part of himself.

> This was Arlington and here they all lay, formed up for the last time. He could almost hear the distant notes of adjutant's call. . . . For a moment, he felt exalted by it, by the thought of all these dead, the history of the nation. . . . He would never lie there; he had given that up long ago. He would never know the days with Jana

again either. He remembered her at that moment as she had been, when she was slender and young. He was loyal to her. It was one-sided but that was enough.

When at the end they had all stood with their hands over their hearts, Newell was to one side, alone, resolutely saluting, faithful, like the fool he had always been.

Alone. Resolute. Faithful. Fool.

That, too, is enough.

The title story, "Last Night," is about a brave and kind action, but then the story becomes harrowing, and then even more harrowing. To say more would give too much away. It is the last story in the collection. If you read the stories in order it would be a good idea to reread immediately "Arlington" or "My Lord You."

AMONG the novels, *Light Years* is a good place to start. The one word that occurs to many readers is "luminous." Richard Ford in his excellent introduction to the Vintage edition writes that the prose is "so luminous, so finely chosen, and balanced that we might not immediately notice that the novel is taking aim at grave matters." I gave *Light Years* to a friend and mentor. He sent back one of his habitually laconic notes: "Luminously depressing." Although I saw what he meant, I disagreed. I was reminded of the split among friends of mine after we all went to see *La Dolce Vita,* one of Fellini's masterpieces. One side was stunned and depressed by how dark it was. The other side was thrilled by how beautiful it was. My friend Tony Winner pitched his tent in both camps. I'm in the Richard Ford camp, the camp that rejoices that Salter writes so beautifully about both the darkness and the light. In other reviews there are more oxymorons:

"Salter celebrates the silver-and-golden bitterness of life."—James Wolcott, *Esquire*

"An absolutely beautiful, monstrous, important book."—Joy Williams

"Icy logic and steaming carnality. . . . Satire worked out of a full heart."—Ned Rorem

At least two of the speakers at Jim's memorial service said that his work celebrates the ecstasies of living and considers how soon it all ends. Sooner or later, there is a thought like this: "It happens in an instant. It is all one long day, one endless afternoon, friends leave, we stand on the shore."

That is Viri, the husband in the book. At his former wife, Nedra's, funeral, one of her daughters, Danny, considers her own children, aged two and four:

Two daughters, one on each side, who, though
they were unaware of it, would know another
century, the millennium. . . . Certainly they
would be passionate and tall and one day give to
their children—there is no assurance of this, we
imagine it, we cannot do otherwise—marvelous
birthdays, huge candle-rich cakes, contests,
guessing games, not many young guests, six or
eight, a room that leads to a garden, from afar one
can hear the laughing, the doors open suddenly,
out they run into the long, sweet afternoon.

This is a tribute. Danny is remembering one of
the good things Nedra and Viri did, one of the gifts
they gave. Danny's thought leaps forward from her
mother to her own children, to her children's children. In the middle of this the narrator intervenes,
casting a shadow: "there is no assurance of this, we
imagine it, we cannot do otherwise." Three phrases,
each a complete sentence, each like the tolling of a
great bell. The first stroke is dull but dire. The second is the fainter note of the backswing, how sweet
but frail it is to *imagine*. The third stroke resounds
more fully: "we cannot do otherwise." To that there
is no answer, unless it is, "All right. We will go on
using our gifts no matter what."

Salter had provisionally titled *Light Years* as *Nedra and Viri* because she was the stronger one. In the end, for all her affairs and scattered interests, she has established the family, the female line. At Nedra's funeral Danny honors her and the vision that has come from her.

IN THE first lecture, "The Art of Fiction," Salter talks of the great works, the great writers: Balzac, Babel, Flaubert, Hemingway. In the third lecture he will add Nabokov, Saul Bellow, and Isaac Bashevis Singer. Salter gives detailed analyses of short passages from each of the four. He remarks, "The writers I like are those who are able to observe closely."

In between the analyses there are confessional notes—Salter's envy when he saw a book by Jack Kerouac in a bookstore window—that's Jack Kerouac who had been a high-schoolmate of Salter's. And Salter's near despair at the bad reviews he got for *Light Years.* I found these reviews hasty, ignorant, and dismissible. That's from afar. Salter was wounded. In this lecture he says, "It's a rare writer who doesn't experience rejection at one point or another, and the book was after all not anything sacred, though it had been sacred to me. But this is philosophically speaking and was of no use at the time. Philosophy is a slow-acting remedy."

After the ability to observe closely, Salter suggests that the next step is style. He then corrects himself—a better word is "voice."

"In the beginning when you start as a writer you usually have no voice. You are usually influenced by or attracted to an established writer. . . . Whatever he does, you try to do. However he regards things, you do the same. But gradually the attachment weakens, and you become attracted to other writers, not so intensely, and your own writing, through its practice, changes, and the time comes when you are writing entirely as yourself, unmediated, and you sound like yourself."

To end the first lecture, Salter turns to Thomas Wolfe, about whom Salter has noted earlier that he "wrote books from which many hundreds of pages had to be cut."

But Salter has a good ear and a good memory for the good things he has read. He finds a gem. It is four lines long, one splendidly unwinding sentence: "Thomas Wolfe wrote a last letter—he was dying— to his first editor, Maxwell Perkins, whom he later forsook. It's in his true romantic voice: 'I shall always think of you and feel about you the way it was that Fourth of July three years ago when you met me at the boat and we went out on the café on the river and had a drink and later went on top of the tall building, and all the strangeness and the glory and the power of life and of the city was below.'"

THERE are many cautions and sighs in the second talk, "How to Write a Novel."

"Actually, I don't think anyone can teach you how to write a novel," Salter says.

He quotes Anthony Powell: "You've got to do a lot of very boring things along the way over a long period, and if you can't do that, all the imagination in the world is no good."

Evelyn Waugh: "If only the amateurs would get it into their heads that novel writing is a highly skilled and laborious trade."

Céline: "You've got to pay. A story you make up, that isn't worth anything. The only story that counts is the one you pay for. When it's paid for, then you've got the right to transform it."

Salter for himself: "You have to write instead of living. You have to give so much to it to get something back. You get only a little back, but it's something. . . . You're doing it all for almost nothing, as in the beginning Justine made love for a cotton shirt."

That's the bad news. Then some good news.

"Voltaire wrote *Candide* as social comment, tossed it off when he was sixty-five."

"Theodore Dreiser was visiting a friend named

Arthur Henry. . . . Henry was working on a novel. Why don't you write one? he suggested to Dreiser. Dreiser sat down and took a sheet of paper and wrote at the top, *Sister Carrie.*"

Salter writes, "Dreiser was a bad writer, repetitious, vulgar, obvious, and untruthful, but he was also a great storyteller, relentless and teeming with ideas." Robert Penn Warren said of Dreiser, "He knew that the filth of self, to be loved, must be clothed in glory."

Along with the bad news and the somewhat better news there are occasional outbursts of pleasure, as when Salter quotes Léataud, a French drama critic whom Salter found of interest. *"Écrire! Quelle chose merveilleuse!"* To write! What a marvelous thing!

There is also a paragraph of Salter's own, ending with a thought from Salter's "final vocabulary." Final vocabulary is a phrase of Richard Rorty's, a philosopher who thought modern philosophy had strayed too far from helpfulness; he advised everyone to work out a final vocabulary, by which he meant the things or ideas that mean the most to each of us.

Why write? Salter confesses to the lesser reasons— pretty much the same ones George Orwell confesses to in his essay "Why I Write." Salter lists "to be admired by others, to be loved by them, to be praised, to be known. . . . *None of those reasons give the strength of the desire.*"

BESIDES the skills of observing closely, besides the love of words, besides the lessons derived from instruction, besides reading and rereading to see how an effect has been achieved, and besides the *desire*, what else might there be? In "Life into Art," the third lecture, Salter includes as answer almost everything, almost anything: an overheard phrase, the way someone crosses the street, an incident in the life of a friend.

Yevgeny Zamyatin is the author of *We*, an anti-utopian novel written in 1924 that foresaw what Soviet Russia would become under Stalin. Zamyatin said in a lecture that when he was full of ideas that hadn't yet taken a unified form, a chance observation often pulled them together. It was, he said, like adding one more crystal to a supersaturated solution: the crystals began to join together coherently.

So it's not surprising that Salter has a similar notion. (How I wish that Zamyatin had come up in our conversations!) Salter says in this third talk, "You don't do all the writing at your desk. You do it elsewhere, carrying the book with you. The book is your companion, you . . . [are] alert for links to it."

But that lucky accident—*apparent* accident—wouldn't do its magic unless you also had the routine, the ritual, the discipline of a writer. Salter says, "I try to write regularly. . . . I write when I don't feel like it, but not when it revulses me. . . . I write by hand with a pen. Then I type it on an electric typewriter. . . . I like the sound, slightly irregular, of the keys hitting."

Salter also mentions in his first lecture or in an aside that Flaubert wrote forty-five hundred pages to get the three hundred of *Madame Bovary*. About his own novel, *All That Is,* he says, "I made two thick notebooks for this book, reference books divided into sections holding things from my journals that might be of some use: weather, places, conversation, faces, deaths, love, sex, people. *Toda*. I didn't use even a quarter of it."

It takes a lot of miles of training to run a race.

But Salter also records how as a young man, after writing imitatively and inconclusively for a long time, he finally wrote a good story. He mentions some details that he noted by chance: a German girl at a *Fasching* ball in a costume "like a bathing suit with gold scales and a skirt." There is a man who drifts by. Another German girl. "The next day we went to the beach. And that's it. That's the story, but the difference this time was that I was able to write it. It was the language, the assurance. I knew only a limited amount about the German girls, but I pressed down hard. . . . I somehow made it count."

That "somehow" is less mysterious in light of these lectures.

THE ART OF FICTION

THE ART OF FICTION

People can be known to faint at the sight of something or upon hearing some news or the voice of someone thought to be long dead, but no one faints upon reading a book. Which is not to say books have no power; they have a different kind of power. You're not seeing or hearing anything as you read, but you believe you are. I believed I was in French Indochina when I was reading Marguerite Duras's *The Lover.* I saw the wide boulevards lined with trees, the white suits, the Chinese quarter. I knew her mother and her brother, the incredible naked body of Hélène Lagonelle, the pathetic lover, and the fact all of it was in the past but also present in the face of the woman who wrote it. The novel is written in the first person. It's a confession and only made up, but I believed it. It became part of my history of the world.

This is something François Mauriac related:

One day, a boy of fifteen, named Paul Bourget, entered a reading room on the rue Soufflet and asked for the first volume of *Père Goriot*. It was one o'clock when he began reading. It was seven when the young Paul was once more in the street having finished the entire work. "The hallucination of that reading was so strong," Bourget wrote, "that I staggered. . . . The intensity of the dream into which Balzac had plunged me produced effects on me similar to those of alcohol or opium. I stayed a few minutes taking in the reality of the things about me and my own poor reality."

Balzac, as you probably know, had written a number of inferior novels under various pseudonyms before he began the epic twenty years of writing under his own name, in the course of which he published some ninety novels, including many masterpieces, of which *Old Goriot* is one.

Certain writers have the ability to put one word with another or together as a sequence that causes it to bloom in the reader's mind or to describe things so well that they become for the reader something close or equal to reality. It's not simply that they are well observed; it's also in the way of telling.

Goriot is an old man, at one time successful and

rich with two beautiful daughters whom he worships and gives everything to, including the arrangement of the most beneficial marriages. It's something like King Lear—he gives them everything and they prove to be ungrateful and supremely selfish. He is not even admitted to their lavish houses now and he lives, impoverished, on the topmost floor of a third-rate boarding house, Maison Vauquer, where he is considered insignificant, yet he is still completely devoted to the uncaring daughters, whom incidentally no one knows about.

Every detail of this boarding house, every room and its furnishings, every occupant is masterfully described, Balzac insisting through these details that All This Is True! This entire story of a venal, glamorous, swarming nineteenth-century Paris, stench hole and stately paradise, is completely true.

So we come into the dining room of Maison Vauquer with its walls of a now unrecognizable color, its chipped and stained decanters, piles of plates on the sticky sideboards, and wine-spattered napkins of the boarders pigeoned in a box. The table is covered with a greasy oilcloth, the grass place mats unraveled almost to the point of disappearance, and the chairs are rickety and broken-backed.

In short, poverty without glamour reigns here, a narrow, concentrated, threadbare poverty. Although actual filth may be absent, everything is dirty and stained; there are no rags and tatters, but everything is falling to pieces with decay.

This room is in all its glory at about seven in the morning when Madame Vauquet's cat appears downstairs, a sign that his mistress is on the way.

In this medley of decline with its procession of details, shifts of focus, the direct address to the reader, the inspired scrutiny, using it all as a kind of fanfare, there is the mock regal entrance of a principal figure, the proprietess herself, Madame Vauquer, shuffling in like an old actress in creased slippers with her tulle cap crooked on her head, a predecessor of our own hairdressers and fallen festival queens. A brilliant page is then given to her description, which I won't quote in full, but which begins with this:

Her ageing puffy face dominated by a nose like a parrot's beak, her dimpled little hands, her body plump as a church rat's, her bunchy shapeless dress are in their proper setting in this room where misery oozes from the walls and hope, trodden down and stifled, has surrendered to despair.

Writers before Balzac had omitted—as being crude and uninteresting—the details of everyday life that he so voraciously assembled and made use of as an essential part of the truth, of reality. He opened the door to this.

I READ for the pleasure of reading. I'm not obliged to read anything anymore, and I don't feel obliged to read anything, although there are certain books I'd like to read before I die, for what reason it's hard to say. I'd somehow feel incomplete otherwise, not quite ready. I would like to read *The Makioka Sisters* by Junichirō Tanizaki. I want to read Miklós Bánffy's *The Transylvanian Trilogy,* and Hermann Broch's *The Sleepwalkers.* I see myself as reading at the end in the way that Edmund Wilson in his last days was learning Hebrew with oxygen tanks at the foot of his bed.

Of course there are always books that, if I don't read, I may examine out of curiosity or to see how they are written. I don't really need to know that, but it's a craving.

Over the years I've never found myself truly intimate or comfortable for a long period with people who don't read or have never read. For me, it's an essential. Something is missing in them otherwise, breadth of reference, sense of history, a common

chord. Books are passwords. Film is too simple. Perhaps I'm wrong. I was in a noisy bar one time and a
man came up to me—this was in my own town—and
said something to me I couldn't hear, then closer to
my ear said again, "What do you think of Neruda?"
I didn't really have an opinion about Neruda, but
something in me warmed at his homely attempt to be
friends. I read Neruda afterwards which I might not
have done, or almost not.

It's impossible to read everything. No matter how
well read a person may be, there remain a great number of both fundamental and less-recognized books
that are going to be unread or ought to be read or,
as a bibliophile friend, Jacques Bonnet, says, are to
be read sometime. And then you are always coming
across interesting-sounding writers you hadn't heard
of. It was because of Bonnet that I read Nagai Kafū,
"The River Sumida," and two or three other writers.
There is too much to read and always will be.

The books I've read and liked I remember quite
well, and there is a kind of relationship formed with
their writers. I think many readers experience this.
If the book is good, the writer himself must be. The
feeling may be one of admiration or infatuation,
sometimes even a kind of worship. I've known too
many writers to think of worshipping them, but I can
understand what others might feel. You are always

being asked for the names of writers you like or have been influenced by, and I never seem to have that list in my pocket, but on it would be some writers that a writer named Robert Phelps introduced me to when I first met him in New York. That would be in 1969. I was forty-four years old and had been living on the outside, not in any sense in a literary life.

As it happened, *The Literary Life* was the title of a book Phelps had written with Peter Deane, a history with photographs of the years from 1900 to 1950 focused entirely on books, literary events, and writers in both their public and private lives. For me it was an irresistible book. I was a writer and I wanted to be in the next volume, the one going from 1950 to 2000, but for several reasons, his death being one of them, Robert Phelps never wrote it. He took me under his wing, however. He provided me my course in comparative literature, which he was also teaching at the New School at that time.

Phelps and his wife, Rosemarie Beck, who was a painter, lived in a small apartment of only two rooms connected by a kitchen. There was their bedroom with a small table at which they sometimes ate, and the other room was a studio, half of which was hers and the other half, carefully delineated, was his. There was only one shelf for books, and it happened to be in her half, and in addition, part of the shelf was hers. So the books he possessed were limited in number, perhaps thirty or thirty-five—the exact number of books on each shelf in the infinite library of Babel that Borges describes as a metaphor for the universe, any of which might be replaced at any time by another book Phelps loved or deemed more worthy. Books that had been displaced and all review copies and books that hadn't even had the chance to be candidates for the bookshelf went to the Strand Bookstore nearby or were stacked in the hall for anyone to take.

The Phelpses' apartment on the topmost floor seemed Parisian to me. Perhaps I was influenced by his work. His sympathies and expertise were focused particularly on French literature. He had done an autobiography of Colette—*Earthly Paradise*—composed of long sections taken from her own fiction and nonfiction books. He also wrote an illustrated biography of her and a more traditional biography of Jean Cocteau. He was published by Farrar, Straus and Giroux, the offices of which were only a few blocks away.

Phelps always referred to Straus, the head of the house, as Roger, and later he began calling him Our Roger when it seemed he might also publish me. At the time I was writing a novel. I was at odds with my wife; we were barely speaking, and I was thinking back to the days when we'd been happy, not so much trying to remember them, but the way in which I remembered them as well as which things I remembered. I was writing about those days of a decade before as they were stacked in me, and in particular the days involving a couple who were our friends, and the wife who fascinated me and who in a gesture I remembered would always remove her wedding ring and place it on the counter when she cooked. I felt I was really writing about her.

Some years later, a woman writer told me that she had loved the book so much that she had a word from it tattooed on her finger where her own wedding ring might be.

What was the word, I asked her.

She showed me her finger.

The word was "inimitable."

Up until the time I met Robert Phelps, everything I knew I had learned by myself. I had formed my tastes by myself, and he refined them by introducing me to new writers and resituating many of the old. I trusted him.

One of the writers he suggested I read—he wrote down the titles of three of his stories for me—was the Russian writer Isaac Babel.

"Read this one first," he said. It was the story called "My First Goose."

I suspect you may know more than I did at the time, but of the existence of a writer such as Babel I simply had no idea. He wrote in the 1920s, short stories and plays, and in 1940 he was executed by the NKVD. His stories are grouped mainly around life in Odessa, where he was a boy, and his accompanying the Red Army during its campaign against the Poles in 1920. It's difficult to describe these stories and the power they have to astonish and move the reader. They have been honed down to a breathtaking intensity.

Babel is an unobtrusive writer. He holds himself back from the story and allows it to conclude itself, often in a staggering way. He's a little man with glasses who is traveling with the Cossack army as a correspondent and is somehow able to look down on the mayhem happening all about him with the forbearance of God—Borges said of his style that it achieved a glory seemingly reserved for poems and rarely attained by prose. He gives all this over to you. It's like a handful of radium—a brilliance you would never imagine.

Babel wrote and rewrote his stories tirelessly. He said that in a sentence there was something like a lever that you could put your hand on and give it a slight, just the right, twist, not too much or too little, and everything would fall into place. You perhaps can't picture that, but you can see it in his sentences.

He also unforgettably said that there was no iron that could pierce the human heart with as much force as a period put in just the right place.

I read Babel's stories again and again. One of them, "Dante Street," is set in Paris. Another is called "Guy de Maupassant" although Maupassant never appears in it. Babel had traveled to Italy and to France a number of times and would have liked to stay longer, but too long abroad made one suspect, and in the end he returned to the Soviet Union. He continued to work but was somewhat marginalized and perhaps too openly freethinking. He was arrested suddenly, imprisoned, and charged with espionage, grave charges against which there was no defense in the Soviet Union, and then one night tried in the cellars and the next day executed. All his unfinished manuscripts and papers were confiscated at the time of his arrest and have never been found.

THE NOVEL that I had been writing, *Light Years*, turned out not to be a success. It was published but had a devastating, followed by a second, indifferent, review in the *Times*, and there was no one interested in trying to defend it. My editor at Random House had called with the news. It was a bad review, he told me.

Really? How bad?

Very bad.

Was there something in it though, some phrase or a couple of words that could be used in an ad?

No, he said.

It's a rare writer who doesn't experience rejection at one point or another, and the book was after all not anything sacred, though it had been sacred to me. But this is philosophically speaking and was of no use at the time. Philosophy is a slow-acting cure.

Of course, there were people who liked the book; there are always some people, and perhaps they are right, but as a rejection, this was the single one most painful to me. I suppose I could have started a regimen of hard work to get myself over it. I could have started another book, but my passion felt spent. I had worked five years on the book. I had used myself up. Instead I went to France, where you can always feel it's worthwhile to be a writer and where I had always been able to write. It's not every writer who likes France. In fact, I think France if anything has been too greatly loved—it begins to be an affect—but I always felt comfortable there.

BABEL never wrote a novel. It's a form he was un-suited for. A novel is, in my view of it, a narrative of some length and succinct only in places. Per-haps it should also have some social matrix or rele-vance, should include life as measured by values, as E. M. Forster said, but I think not necessarily.

In the last two hundred years, during which it has become the dominant literary genre, novelists have generally been the most important literary figures. Orhan Pamuk, inspired by an influential essay of Schiller's, "On Naïve and Sentimental Poetry," has divided writers into those two classes, the naïve and the sentimental. By naïve, he means writers who are natural, like springs, spontaneous—without aware-ness of how they are writing, it pours forth—and he lists under this category Dante, Shakespeare, Cer-vantes, Sterne, and Goethe. The sentimental writers on the other hand are faced with various problems of style and technique and would seem, as a conse-quence, a step away from the more blessed, like hard-working, slower students. This group would have to include Tolstoy, Gogol, Virginia Woolf, Thomas Mann, and almost everyone else. It would certainly include, at the top of the list, Flaubert.

Flaubert began writing *Madame Bovary* in 1851, a year after Balzac died. He was nearly thirty years old. He admired Balzac; they were both realists. *Madame*

Bovary, which was to become the iconic realist novel, took four and a half years to write. Where the idea for the novel came from, how much was based on an actual case or case history, are interesting subjects, but I'd like to talk about Flaubert and his methods, his manner of working and his hopes and intentions.

Flaubert was a bachelor. He never married. He lived all his life in a comfortable family house with a large garden overlooking the river in Croisset, a place near Rouen. There were servants. He lived with his mother and a young niece, Caroline, to whom he was devoted. He traveled rarely, sometimes to Paris to get away or to see friends, and once with Maxime Du Camp, a friend, to Egypt. It was a completely bourgeois life though he scorned the bourgeois. The slime of the bourgeois, he said, and their democratic society. He had a lover, a poet, Louise Colet, but she lived in another town, and so he was able to focus his energy entirely on his work.

His study was upstairs, a large room with a view over the garden down to the Seine. He usually wrote in this room from early afternoon into early morning, stopping only for dinner, and he was tireless, writing, rewriting, revising, and slowly producing perhaps "a page a week or one in four days or thirteen in three months." There are some forty-five hundred pages of drafts for the three hundred in the book.

He weighed each sentence. He selected, rejected, reselected each word. "A good sentence in prose," he said, "should be like a good line in poetry, un-changeable, as rhythmic, as sonorous." He tested his sentences and paragraphs aloud in what he called his *gueuloir*—his yelling place—to judge their rhythm and fluidity. He also ritually read aloud to a friend what he had written each week.

He wanted to write objectively, exactly, precisely, withholding metaphor and moral judgment. Above all he wanted to write a novel that was realistic, al-most clinical, not romanticizing, and to make some-thing monumentally beautiful out of provincial peo-ple and commonplace, even shallow lives. It would all depend on style. The style of the writing was of pri-mary importance. He even went so far as to say that "it would be a book about nothing . . . depending on nothing external . . . held together by the external strength of its style." But of course, it's more than that; it's a miraculous gift of a complete world.

In the novel, Rodolphe, the dark-haired, mascu-line landowner who is Emma Bovary's seducer, has drawn her up into an empty council room where they can sit looking down on the agricultural fair going on below.

He sat with his arms crossed over his knees, and, lifting his face towards Emma, he looked at her fixedly from very near. She could distinguish in his eyes little lines of gold radiating out all around his black pupils, and she could even smell the scent of the pomade with which his hair was glazed. Then a languor came over her; she recalled the vicomte who had waltzed with her at La Vaubyessard, whose beard had given off the same smell of vanilla and lemon as this hair; and reflexively she half closed her eyelids the better to breathe it in.

I want to pause here. She could see the little lines of gold, smell the scent of pomade, and remember the vicomte's beard that had given off the same fateful smell of lemon and vanilla. She half closed her eyelids. Even so small a detail—half closed her eyelids, not her eyes. It's more tender. It intimates a white curtain, something graceful and fine to match the languor and recall.

But as she did this, straightening in her chair, she saw in the distance, on the farthest horizon, the old stagecoach, the *Hirondelle,* slowly descending the hill of Les Leux, trailing a long plume of dust behind it. It was in that yellow carriage that Léon had so often returned to her; and by that very road he had left forever! She believed she could see him across the square, at his window; then everything blurred together, a few clouds passed; it seemed to her that she was still circling in the waltz, under the blaze of the chandeliers, in the arms of the vicomte, and that Léon was not far off, that he was coming . . . and yet she could still sense Rodolphe's head next to her. And so the sweetness of this sensation permeated her desires of earlier times, and like grains of sand lifted before a gust of wind, they whirled about in the subtle whiff of the fragrance that was spreading throughout her soul.

So, although she is only half seeing it, small as a fingernail in the distance, there is the slight touch of yellow that draws her into the past. But this is only the beginning. The scene goes on, becoming more and more intense, hallucinatory, and is counterpointed by the novelist leaving them and describing the scene below which they are barely looking at, where a medal is being awarded to a simple old woman who has been a worker on a farm, like a beast of burden, for more than fifty years and now is being given a silver medal. We can actually see this small, frightened woman with her thin, wrinkled face and two long hands with gnarled joints.

Barn dust, caustic washing soda, and wool grease had so thoroughly encrusted, chafed, and hardened them that they seemed dirty even though they had been washed in clear water: and from the habit of serving, they remained half open, as though offering their own testimony to the great suffering they had endured.

She receives the medal. She studies it. At last a beatific smile spreads over her plain face.

"I'll give it to the curé," she murmurs, "so that he will say some masses for me."

Style. Flaubert wanted objectivity and style, the exact choice of the right word. Speech is a natural human attribute and for the most part comes forth easily, almost willy-nilly, but writing is not the same. Writing is more difficult.

Maupassant was Flaubert's pupil, I mean literally. They knew one another, and Flaubert taught Maupassant how to write, how it was done. Maupassant brought his first story to Flaubert—I believe this is true—to have his judgment of it. It was called *"Boule de suif"*—"ball of fat"—and Maupassant was extremely nervous. He was twenty-nine years old. Was it any good or not? When Flaubert had read it, he gave it back. He said only, "It's a masterpiece." Then he added, "I would only change two words."

Of course, not every word can be the perfect word. Not every room overlooks the river. There are thousands of ordinary words that make up a book, just as in an army there are many ordinary soldiers and occasional heroes. But there should not be wrong words or words that degrade the sentence or page. You have to have a taste for what you're writing. You have to be able to recognize when it's gone bad.

There actually might not *be* a right word, much less the perfect one. You might have to change your mind and do it with two words or rewrite the sentence. Not every book is worth doing that for, for every sentence, every paragraph. Not every writer does it. There are degrees of good.

But style can be something else. Style is the entire writer. You can be said to have a style when a reader, after reading several lines or part of a page, can recognize who the writer is. Flaubert sought to remove himself from his book entirely, to have it exist without him, as if his attitudes were not a part of it, his sense of irony, his taste. But he can't be removed from the book—there is something else. I feel a resistance to the word "style" because it can also suggest something inessential like "ornament" or "fashion."

I sometimes prefer the word "voice" instead. They are not exactly the same thing. Style is a preference; a voice is almost genetic, absolutely distinctive. No other writer sounds like Isak Dinesen. No one sounds like Raymond Carver or Faulkner. They rewrite endlessly: Babel, Flaubert, Tolstoy, Virginia Woolf. To be a writer is to be sentenced to correcting. It wasn't what they intended to write. Or it was but the intention was misguided, or it could be better; it was too long, it was flat; it missed the true point, it didn't look right. But it always sounds like them. It's their style. It's in their voice.

In the beginning when you start as a writer you usually have no voice. You are usually influenced by or attracted to an established writer, someone whose books and aura dazzle you. Whatever he does, you try to do. However he regards things, you do the same. But gradually the attachment weakens, and you become attracted to other writers, not so intensely, and your own writing, through its practice, changes, and the time comes when you are writing entirely as yourself, unmediated, and you sound like yourself.

Style is substance—so Nabokov said, and his own style demonstrated it. He wrote the way he spoke, only better.

Then there is the first time you read the opening

words of a book and feel a kind of warning, an electricity running through you, the same as with sex.

> In the late summer of that year we lived in a house in a village that looked across the river and the plain to the mountains. In the bed of the river there were pebbles and boulders, dry and white in the sun, and the water was clear and swiftly moving and blue in the channels. Troops went by the house and down the road and the dust they raised powdered the leaves of the trees. The trunks of the trees too were dusty and the leaves fell early that year and we saw the troops marching along the road and the dust rising and leaves, stirred by the breeze, falling and the soldiers marching and afterward the road bare and white except for the leaves.

As Joan Didion said of it, the sentences dictate "a certain way of looking at the world, a way of looking but not joining, a way of moving through but not attaching, a kind of romantic individualism distinctly adapted to its time and place." The time was 1929, although the action of the novel takes place in 1917, the next to last year of the First World War and the year of Italian military disaster.

A certain way of looking at things and a way to express it. The paragraph is written in words of one and sometimes two syllables, very simple words, words of nature: river, plain, pebbles, trees, dust. Native words. It is primal language, the language of a better and somehow truer world, repetitive for effect and almost liturgical with its frequent conjunctions, a hallmark of Hemingway's writing. The leaves fall . . . *and* we saw . . . *and* the dust . . . *and* leaves . . . *and* the soldiers . . . *and* afterward—afterward, a word of three syllables. It's realism, but with a bias. It's a voice as well as a style. Hemingway was a sentimental writer, at least according to Pamuk's classification. Words don't simply pour out of him, as for example they poured out of Jack Kerouac and Thomas Wolfe, who wrote books from which many hundreds of pages had to be cut.

I WAS in Pensacola one afternoon—this was after the war—walking along the street when I stopped to look in a bookshop window. There was a book with a bold-looking jacket called *The Town and the City*. The author's name stood out for me: John Kerouac. I knew a Jack Kerouac who I'd been in high school with and who wrote stories then. Could this be him?

I went in and picked up the book. There was a photograph on the back. I recognized him immediately. I was stunned. He'd been a year ahead of me at school and all his friends had been a year ahead. He was stocky and athletic, a fast runner. He played football. I'd heard he went on to Columbia to play. I read a few pages of the book and bought it and took it home.

"This was written by Jack Kerouac," I said, showing it to my wife. She didn't know him—I hadn't met her until long after school. I explained who he was, but I didn't explain how I felt on seeing his book—envious, even sick with envy, outdone.

My wife wasn't particularly sympathetic to my interest in writing. She didn't oppose it; she was indifferent to it. But I'd been walking in uniform on a street in Pensacola and suddenly had seen the image of something other than the life I was living.

The Town and the City were Lowell, Massachusetts—Kerouac's hometown—and New York, where he met the main figures in his life, William Burroughs, Allen Ginsberg, Neal Cassady, and also several of his wives. The writing is heavily influenced by Thomas Wolfe. I'd read Thomas Wolfe, the three huge novels, his long, exuberant descriptions of the mundane and his unappeasable self, his search for meaning and love, sometimes ending in the iambic, Mrs. Jack—Esther Jack—he plucked her from life. It was this exuberance that Kerouac found in him and that became a power to blow elegy like jazz. I read

The Town and the City; I was moved deeply by the fact that it had been written.

I had never written a novel although I had tried. I had written a few stories. Eventually I wrote a much longer one and showed it to a good friend. He and his fiancée read it and advised me to tear it up. It's humbling to write about yourself and have it ridiculed. Of course, I had pretended it wasn't about me, but you could see it on every page.

I don't know where the urge to write comes from. I don't believe it's inborn, but it comes early. I had no daemon in me, as Faulkner said he had, or D. H. Lawrence, but there are writers who have no daemon. I don't think Ford Madox Ford did. John Updike had no daemon. Lampedusa didn't. In any case, genius is unto itself. What I had was merely a desire that might well have lasted just so long. Then a sympathetic figure appeared for me. He was an agent who had been for a long time a magazine editor and who took me on although I had nothing that had been published and nothing to show apart from that one attempt, but I had worked more on that, and he felt it was good enough to submit.

In my other life, I had got put into flying transports. It was boring, but you're young; the names of distant places mean something to you. Nobody thought there would be a war; that was over with.

This was in 1946, four years before the Korean War that suddenly broke like a storm, it seemed overnight. By the time that happened I was in fighters and eager to go. It would be foolish to get killed in them and not have it be in the war. It was operatic, saying goodbye and carrying a fear that you wouldn't come back—never confessing it.

Sometime during this I received a note from my agent: *Harper's* had rejected the manuscript, but the editor had said, in turning it down, If he writes another book, we'd be interested in seeing it. So I was a writer at last. Or would be perhaps in five years. That was how long it took between the time I began again and when I finished.

The novel I began was *The Hunters*. I knew from the first what its style would be but not its form. I couldn't find that despite thinking of it all the time and even almost seeing it—that is to say imagining it as being written. Then one day it came. I sat down and wrote on the blank area of a map the outline in chapters of the book. It was accepted and I also received a contract for another.

THE WRITERS I like are those who are able to observe closely. Details are everything. My aims in writing are not that far from Flaubert's: realism, objectivity, and style. Sentences that go together as if that were their only purpose but are not there for their own sake. At one time I felt I would like to write a book of perfect pages, but I came to think that was too constraining. I still attach great importance to style. It seems to me that style is what endures.

We went not long ago, my wife and I, to visit Flaubert's grave in Rouen. It was a pilgrimage, I suppose—I've made a number of them, not so much in homage as simply to be there and think. Willa Cather's grave is beautiful. It's in New Hampshire in a place called Jaffrey Center, where she used to spend summers. It has a line on it from *My Antonía: That is happiness, to be dissolved into something complete and great.*

Flaubert's grave is modest; it is virtually hidden away among others, a stone with nothing more inscribed on it than Here lies Gustave Flaubert, born in Rouen, and the dates. His true monument, of course, is everywhere.

Thomas Wolfe wrote a last letter—he was dying—to his first editor, Maxwell Perkins, whom he later forsook. It's in his true romantic voice.

> I shall always think of you and feel about you
> the way it was that Fourth of July three years
> ago when you met me at the boat, and we went
> out on the café on the river and had a drink and

later went on top of the tall building, and all the strangeness and the glory and the power of life and of the city was below.

I think I'll stop here.
I plan next time to talk about how to write a novel.

WRITING NOVELS

Novels are longer than stories, and it's because of this length, I'm going to say amplitude, that they have the chance—it's actually an obligation—to be more complex and probably involve more characters, call them people. Most novels are narrative, that is to say linear in form and faithful to chronology, going forward in time or folded back and forth in it. The narrative tells a story, and story is at the heart of things. It's the fundamental element. E. M. Forster in *Aspects of the Novel,* which is English and slightly old-fashioned, talks of the importance of telling a story and the skills of one of its most brilliant practitioners, the vizier's clever daughter, Scheherazade:

> Great novelist though she was, exquisite in her descriptions, tolerant in her judgments, ingenious in her incidents, advanced in her morality, vivid in her delineation of character, expert in her

knowledge of three oriental capitals—it was yet
on none of these gifts that she relied when trying
to save her life from her intolerable husband.
They were but incidental. She only survived
because she managed to keep the king wondering
what would happen next. Each time she saw the
fun rising she stopped in the middle of a sentence
and left him gaping. At this moment Scheherazade saw the morning appearing and, discreet,
was silent.

That last phrase, as Forster notes, is the backbone
of *The Thousand and One Nights:* Scheherazade fell
silent. What came next? The desire to know that is
the engine of literature: Please, go on with the story.

Plot is something more than story. It includes the
causal elements and the surprises. The story of *Lolita* is straightforward: Humbert discovers Lolita, he,
let us say, seduces her, installs her as his pretended
daughter, a somewhat odious but intoxicating situ-
ation, and she is stolen away by a rival. He pursues,
finds them, and shoots the thief. But it is the plot
with its many comic elements, gradual revelation of
motives, and grotesque incidents that elevates everything. *Lolita* was at first misunderstood, as well it
might be, and was saved from likely obscurity or existence on the dirty-book shelf by Graham Greene,

who had it on his list in the *Times* as one of the three best books of the year, thus putting literary approval behind it. Nabokov at the time was a little-known writer.

I'm going to try to talk now about novel writing, but I should say in advance it may not be about the novel you are thinking of writing, or have started to write, or perhaps have half finished. It's really about certain people's novels. It doesn't presume to teach much about how to do it.

Actually, I don't think anyone can teach you how to write a novel, or if they can, not in an hour. It's difficult to write novels. You have to have the idea and the characters, although additional characters may appear to you as you go. You need the story. You need, if I can put it this way, the form: What length book will it be? Written in long paragraphs? Short ones? In which person? A book that is focused or going off in all directions? How dense? When you have the form, you can write the novel. When you have the style. The style. Where you as a writer stand. Your prejudices. Your moral position. The way this book should be read. And after that you need a beginning. "Two mountain chains traverse the republic from north to south . . . ," the subdued first words of the Consul's final ordeal in *Under the Volcano*. The beginning is extremely important. I mentioned the beginning of

A Farewell to Arms previously. It's all in those open-ing sentences: the war from which they are standing apart, or fleeing. They're sheltered for the moment, it's marching past, but their fate is bound up with it.

One of the most difficult things, García Márquez said, was the first paragraph. He had spent months on a first paragraph, he said, but when he got it, the rest was easy. He had the style, the tone, but the problem was how to start to convey it? The first paragraph was a sample of what the rest of the book would be.

The beginning—how it starts. After that, writ-ten either in or out of order, comes the rest, scene by scene, page by page. It's a long task. As a writer you are continually confronted with the need to vi-sualize a scene or a sequence or feeling and then, as completely as you can, write it down. There are many failed attempts at this, pulling this sometimes inex-pressible thing out of yourself. The thing has many aspects, too many, and at least one of them must fi-nally be set down in some linear way, word by word, to the point of your almost losing interest in it. There are always too many choices or there are none, no possible way. In the beginning you can write any-where, but you have to use your real time to write, you have to write instead of living. You have to give so much to it to get something back. You get only a little back, but it's something. There are no established values; you give a lot for nothing; you're doing it all for almost nothing, as in the beginning Justine made love for a cotton shirt.

If it's really this, if it's this difficult to do and for almost everyone very little to be gained by it, little money . . . Well, it is actually a way of earning money; you don't need anything to start with but words. But what is the urge? Why does one write? That's the essence of it. Why, then?

Well, really for pleasure, although it's clear it's not such great pleasure. Then, to please others. I've written with that in mind sometimes, thinking of certain people, but it would be truer to say that I've written to be admired by others, to be loved by them, to be praised, to be known. In the end, that's the only reason. The result is barely related to it. None of those reasons give the strength of the desire.

I always think of Paul Léautaud, an old theater critic, impoverished, almost forgotten. At the end, living alone with a dozen cats, he wrote, *"Écrire!"*— to write—*"Quelle chose merveilleuse!"*

You're the hero of your own life—it belongs to you alone, and it's often the basis for a first novel. No story is more readily at your disposal. Philip Roth wrote his first book, *Goodbye, Columbus,* about himself and an early love affair with a girl in New Jersey.

That segment of his life is the story and its complications form the plot.

Voltaire wrote *Candide* as social comment, tossed it off when he was sixty-five.

Theodore Dreiser was visiting a friend named Arthur Henry in the summer of 1899 in Maumee, Ohio. Henry was working on a novel. Why don't you write one, he suggested to Dreiser? Dreiser sat down and took a sheet of paper and wrote at the top, *Sister Carrie.*

Dreiser came from a family of ten children living in poverty in Warsaw, Indiana. A kind school teacher had paid for him to go to college, which he did not finish. Two of his sisters in the course of things became pregnant or had run off. Dreiser became a bill collector in the Chicago slums, but he had an observant and greedy eye and was stimulated by things he read in papers. He submitted pieces to one of them and before long became a successful writer, then a magazine editor and newspaperman. He was twenty-eight when he began to write *Sister Carrie.* He had no plan at all, no idea of what it would be about. He merely reached back into his life and allowed memory to arrange things with barely a tremor. It took four months to write the book including giving it up after deciding it was rotten. But he had little to lose. *Carrie* was published in a world of fiction the accepted motif of which was virtue assailed but in the end triumphant. It was quickly pulled from publication on moral grounds. Dreiser knew a world of greater reality and the harsh commercialism of many cities, Chicago, St. Louis, Pittsburgh, New York. He had read Nietzsche, Balzac, and Zola and was mesmerized by vague ideas of a superman, and by the god of money and the money kings. "He knew that the filth of self, to be loved, must be clothed in glory," Robert Penn Warren said, and that ambition burned in him all his life. He missed the Nobel Prize, which was awarded to Sinclair Lewis instead. Dreiser was a bad writer, repetitious, vulgar, obvious, and untruthful, but he was also a great storyteller, relentless and teeming with ideas. He was also the first American writer from the wrong side of the tracks. Samuel Clemens was, too, but in a different way.

Why am I saying so much about Dreiser, who is a powerful, over-large presence who believes that the materialist base of life is the underlying truth? It's not for that. The books he wrote so nearly approximate the life he led, of cities, bars, restaurants, and brothels, success and failure, fear of not making it, that it's difficult to know what he added to make it fiction. What is significant is his vision of the order of things, his knowledge of life at the bottom seeking to move upwards through intractable levels of society, seeking a place.

John O'Hara was a doctor's son, but he always felt he had come from the wrong side of the tracks. He was deeply sensitive about not having gone to Princeton or Yale, about being "other." He was a newspaperman and developed, like Dreiser, the habit of close observation to go with an unromanticized knowledge of human behavior. Facility in writing and a sense of story are the benefits, also, of a life in journalism. In O'Hara's short stories there are hundreds of characters, and often he wouldn't bother to know or describe them that well. His method was to put a sheet of paper in his typewriter and think of two faces— he might have seen them on the train, and knowing nothing about them he would put them together in a restaurant or on an airplane and let them begin to talk, small talk at first for a page or two, and they would start to come to life. It was all through dialogue. As they talked, one of them and then the other would say something so revealing that from then on it was only a question of how deeply he wanted to interest himself in their characters. He was a brilliant writer of dialogue and adept at insult and social nuance—where you stood on the social scale—and stories came freely to him.

When it came to his novels, O'Hara was conscientious about characters in them, doing them fully. All the details of their person are there, clothes and perhaps even the stores the clothes came from, the habits, virtues, faults. You get a very complete picture—you can actually see it—the state trooper's leather holster and gloves, his hat, where he parked his car and why, also whom he kowtows to and who he knows the sordid facts about. You see all the society O'Hara is describing and you shiver a little at what will be the result of these deep prejudices and unexpected remarks.

ARE THESE people, these personages, taken from life? Are they based, physically and otherwise, on real people? Are their actions and some of their speech or habits of speech drawn from life? I think you know—although there is always among writers a kind of sensitivity about this, as if taking them from life, admitting it, is a renunciation of art—many or most characters in fiction of course are taken from life, or largely taken. The briefest investigation can end any question of it. Saul Bellow said he based characters on real people but that he always added something. He gave them a little more esprit, he said. In a copy of a book that Colum McCann signed for an auction of first editions, beside the disclaimer that is always printed proclaiming that the book is a work of fiction, the names, characters, places, and incidents are the product of the author's imagination, or are used fictitiously, and that any resemblance to actual events, locales, or persons, living or dead, is entirely coincidental, beside this McCann wrote simply, "Bullshit."

Writers have always taken what they needed and sometimes more than they needed. Circumstances determined what the outcome was. Some people are flattered to be in a book, depending on the portrayal, of course. Some might resent or be outraged to have a presumed version of themselves before the public, great political figures aside. There is a right of satire.

I based the character of the self-seeking pilot in *The Hunters* on that of a known lieutenant, and it was certain that he read the book. Years later, more than sixty, the fact-checker at the *New Yorker* found him listed at a number in Florida, and she called.

Hello, a noncommittal voice said.

Hello. Are you James Low?

Yes, who's this?

She was the fact-checker at the *New Yorker*, she said. She just wanted to ask him a couple of questions.

I'm just mixing a martini, he said. Go right ahead.

I'd like to know, are you the James Low who flew in Korea?

Yes.

Do you know James Salter?

Is *he* still alive? Low said.

COMPOSING a novel is a long process—people and places—and it's not possible to hold all of it in one's head. There are too many details. "You do have to have enormous staying power as a novelist," Anthony Powell said. "You've got to do a lot of very boring things over a long period, and if you can't do that, all the imagination in the world is no good." It was a question of guts. "Like almost everything else in life," he said.

You have to keep track of many things, even apart from who is where and what has happened. Have you said this before? Have you neglected to write that? Have you used this particular word too much? Depending on the word, once in a book may be enough. Inevitably there are notes tacked to the wall or taped to an outline.

John Masters, a novelist who had been a general in the Indian army, wrote on a large index card the biography and description of every character in his book so that he could summon them at any time and they would be consistent. Céline, when he lived in Meudon in the outskirts of Paris after the war, worked at a kitchen table that had a clothesline strung above it. On the clothesline he hung the chapters of the book he was writing. He was a ruined man by that time. He had been imprisoned after the war for collaboration with the Nazis. He had been declared a national disgrace.

In the 1930s, Céline was the dazzling star—meteor, really, almost off the scale of brilliance—after the publication of *Journey to the End of the Night* followed by *Death on the Installment Plan*. He had been wounded in the First World War, and gone to medical school afterwards. He became a doctor and worked in clinics for the poor. He had a strong sense of idealism and sympathy for the ordinary man and his honesty is convincing. He also was fanatically anti-Semitic—his prewar pamphlets are now impossible to find a copy of they are so vile.

But he had invented a new style of writing, an assault of language, withering bursts of it including vulgarity and street slang, obscenity, invective, all of it separated by repeated ellipses, three periods, dot dot dot. I've talked of style. Ideas were nothing, Céline said. If you wanted ideas, the encyclopedias were filled with ideas. The same with messages, meanings. *Ce n'est pas mon domaine, les idées, les messages. . . . Je suis un homme à style.* His was a new voice and a brilliant new style. It was bitter and misanthropic, nihilistic, a death dance, idealism and extreme cynicism intertwined. He wrote in the first person. There was no release from it, and its daring made it strangely liberating, and the hyperbole made it comic.

In *Death on the Installment Plan*, the principal character, Ferdinand, is waiting for a train in the Gare du Nord and is embraced by his mother.

> I was terribly ashamed[. . . .] She hugged me so hard, with such a storm of emotion, that I reeled . . . On those occasions the tenderness that welled up from her misshapen carcass had the strength of a horse . . . The idea of parting drenched her in advance. A howling tornado turned her inside out, as if her soul were coming out her behind, her eyes, her belly, her bosom . . . it hit me in all directions, it lit up the whole station . . . [. . .] I didn't dare to admit it, but in a way I was curious . . . I'd have liked to know how far she could go in her effusions . . . From what nauseating depths was she digging up all this slop?

Ferdinand has never been redeemed. He remains officially outside. He's the convicted murderer that women cannot help being in love with, too deadly to know.

Céline felt that you had to pay for what you wrote; you didn't get it for nothing. "You've got to pay. A story you make up, that isn't worth anything. The only story that counts is the one you pay for. When it's paid for, then you've got the right to transform it."

And nihilism has its cost.

"A time comes when you are all alone," Céline wrote long before it actually happened to him, "when you've come to the end of everything that can happen to you. It's the end of the world, even grief, your own grief, doesn't answer you anymore, and you have to retrace your steps, to go back among people, it makes no difference who."

There is an impression, formed by the friendship or close location of groups of writers, that talents stimulate one another and work benefits from mutual engagement and suggestion. This is probably more true of painters, but in any event it does not fit the case of Céline, who set out alone, actually on travels to Africa and, after the war, to the United States, and who ended alone.

BOOKS that are important weren't written to be important, generally. They became such. By important, I mean so-deemed. Referred to. I can't think that *The Catcher in the Rye* was written as an important, life-altering or significant, book. I believe that it was simply heartfelt. *To Kill a Mockingbird* doesn't bear marks of an intended importance although I don't know what Harper Lee actually felt. Fitzgerald thought all his books were important. *The Great Gatsby* was a short book, only 214 pages, and he was insistent that the publisher sell it at the same price as his longer ones. *The Magic Mountain* seems a book that was written with its importance well in mind, especially knowing Thomas Mann. *Death in Venice*, certainly: the aging writer, Aschenbach, his rectitude and discipline, the beautiful youth Tadzio, fourteen, the son of an aristocratic Polish family. *Death in Venice* is a philosophical book, serious, darkly poetic— love and death, the two greatest primal subjects. Aschenbach never so much as speaks to, much less touches, the young boy. Byron's Venice, Eleanora Duse's Venice, the small sunlit squares, and canal by canal the great palaces floating by, silent gondolas, the deep blacks. Aschenbach realized he "was meant" to go there and, subconsciously realizing it, in erotic dismay, to die. You cannot help thinking of John O'Hara's novel *Appointment in Samarra*, another place where fate sends you unknowing to meet death.

Every story, as Flaherty said, is the theme of its location.

Capote's *In Cold Blood* unrolls in the wheat fields of Kansas. There is a central figure, the detective, and there was the actual crime. Capote happened to read an account of it, relatively brief, in the newspaper. It intrigued him. It was shocking, not more terrible than other ordinary crimes, but it seemed more of a violation—a farmhouse entered during the night and the occupants murdered one by one, the last of them, the young daughter, having heard the shotgun blasts and knowing what they meant, lying there as the two men came upstairs to her. Capote had the beginning, and the book was written as the investigation itself proceeded, which provided the plot—story more than plot. It's all true and also true that it reads more like a novel than a case history. It has a novel's tone and rhythms. Part of the fascination is that the book is being written without an ending, going ahead on daring, as in Joyce saying, "Chance provides me with what I need." But luckily there came an ending, unexpectedly; the murderers were found. And there is a further ending, emotionally powerful, when the writer attends their execution in all its chilling procedure, and his sympathy for them bleeds over into ours.

Alexandria, the city, is the essential element of Durrell's four novels. The city is sunlit, ancient, without urgency, and past any hope of knowing, but its history and legend hold you. The characters, even by their names—Justine, Balthazar, Nessim, and Mountolive—can be nowhere but in this backwa-

ter of the ancient world. Balthazar has come out of
the Bible. Mountolive, too. Nessim is the name of a
prince. And Cavafy himself is the old poet, the poet
of the city as he is called.

Saul Bellow's novels come out of Chicago, an-
nouncing it in advance: "I am an American, Chicago
born." "Know me that way if you want to know me,"
Augie March boasted. The family had come down
from Canada, where Bellow's father was a bootlegger.
They lived on Cortez Street on the second floor, and
"Next door was the boy I had in mind when I was
writing *Augie March*," Bellow said. It was a Chicago
where you worked in bakeries and had a small wood
and coal business, and a twenty-one-year-old Bellow
sat writing at a bridge table in the back bedroom of
his mother-in-law's apartment.

There is Lübeck in all its solid mercantile dignity
in *Buddenbrooks,* and Quauhnahuac of cantines and
tortuous streets in *Under the Volcano.* These places
are not mere locales; they are a preordination of
buildings, streets, and names that become a familiar
reality to you and that exist nowhere else.

You can't return to them, these places, because
they have disappeared, like the great river cities of
India that arose and then vanished after a thousand
years, although these have only been transformed
into shopping malls, chromium and glass, and chain

hotels. Well, that may not apply to Egypt, which is changeless.

I mentioned Léataud, a feared critic and guardian of standards, severe in his judgments. Eventually he fell behind the times and became an anachronism. He became an old man living with cats, disreputable-looking in what seemed pauper's clothes. He also became, at the end, very unexpectedly a kind of celebrity, restored even if only briefly by television. His diaries, published after his death, run to many hundreds of pages and were much awaited because Léautaud was malicious and indiscrete and it was known that they contained erotic details of the weekly visits of his longtime mistress and scourge, Marie Caggiac. As I remember, he called her the Panther.

I don't remember why I was interested in Léautaud other than because of his story, but I started to read the diaries—they were in French, of course—and I still have them on the shelves somewhere. I also began reading at the same time the somewhat more interesting *Memoirs of the Duc de Saint-Simon*, but finally you can have only so much interest in the transactions at the court of Louis XIV at Versailles or the world of Paris intellectuals before the war.

We're friends with Wally Shawn, the playwright and actor, and his wife, Deborah Eisenberg, and a few years ago happened to ask if they knew a certain restaurant that was near us, around the corner on Forty-Sixth Street, in the theater district.

Know it? We used to go there all the time. The most powerful man in New York always ate there. We were terrified to just walk by his table.

The most powerful man, who was that? Mafia?

Frank Rich, they said.

Frank Rich?

He was the chief theater critic for the *Times*.

You were afraid of Frank Rich?

He absolutely controlled New York, they said. He could kill you.

I don't know if Léautaud was that powerful, but he said a number of things that have stayed in my mind. One of them was, Know how to select. He also said, Your language is your country. I've thought about that a great deal, and I may have it backwards—your country is your language. In either case it has a similar meaning. Either that your true country is not geographical but lingual, or that you are really living in a language, presumably your mother tongue. Your life loyalty, as contrasted to your patriotic loyalty, is to language.

I respect language, probably over-respect it. I'm susceptible to it, and I think I remember in language as well as in the images that infuse memory, actually comprise memory and are able to come so fast and replace each other so instantaneously that if they had any physical presence they would be numbing, but they have no presence other than neural and in most ways are beyond our power to control.

In any case, How to select.

Writers have an affinity with painters. For myself, I like to go and look at pictures and think, as I do, of what I am writing or might write. With painters, first of all, it's their perception of things. And then what they choose, sometimes as if unconcernedly, to paint. I always think I should attempt more, looking at the many studies and sketches done for a major work, the enormous preparation and testing of ideas, out of which, in one form or another, comes the painting. With landscape, of course, there is the absolute, unalterable depiction of a real place, which you also may *see* in a novel, though on a different level of seeing.

The backgrounds, too, when you look at them, are instructive, sometimes remarkably plain. You didn't notice it because the picture was made so that your attention never went to the background. It was carried off without your even noticing.

There is the color, the *blue*—I have to stress the word—the unbelievable blue of the couch in Manet's pastel of his mother. There is the red of Matisse's red room. It's not that particular things come to you or are suggested by colors, but you are somehow more open to them. The white horse of Gauguin's is green.

Then there is what they steal, borrow, adapt from each other. Early Gauguin looks like Pissarro or Sisley, Seurat looks like Pissarro, Van Gogh like Utrillo.

And how careful one must be of the sugary, the sweet. How cloying it can be.

You look at pictures in silence, which is a help.

WRITING novels is difficult.

I've mentioned the matter of choices. A writer whom, if forewarned, you might be cautious in approaching, Evelyn Waugh, explained:

> If only the amateurs would get it into their heads that novel writing is a highly skilled and laborious trade. One does not just sit behind a screen jotting down other people's conversation. One has for one's raw material every single thing one has ever seen or heard or felt, and one has to go over that vast smouldering rubbish heap of experience, half-stifled by the fumes and dust, scraping and delving until one finds a few discarded valuables. Then one has to assemble these tarnished and dented fragments, polish them, set them in order and try to make a coherent and significant

arrangement of them. It is not merely a matter of filling up a dustbin haphazardly and emptying it out again.

The aim of every writer, Cyril Connolly said, was to write a masterpiece, and every great while someone does, to the sorrow of other writers who believe that there are only a certain number of real masterpieces and now somebody has gone off with another of them.

I meant to talk about the Albany of William Kennedy and his novel *Legs,* and also about the endings in books. John Irving always writes the last line, has it, before he begins to write, and he says he writes toward that line. I had meant to talk a little about James Jones and the writing school he founded with Lowney Handy, but I really feel that for the moment I've said enough.

LIFE INTO ART

In Bertolt Brecht's diaries he writes about such things as the essence of art, which he describes as simplicity, grandeur, and sensitivity, and its form, coolness.

Looking through the journals that I kept through the heart, so to speak, of my writing life, from 1962 on, I don't find much of this sort of conclusion. There are more names than ideas, not necessarily well-known names and sometimes names that I don't recognize—Iris Gazelle, who could that be? Jay Julian. There are good descriptions and a lot of conversation—talk—but less than I would expect about writing—what I was writing, what I *felt* about something I'd written. The journals themselves are written *comme ça*. They're meant to be used, not read by anyone. Some pages are written with more care, things I would regret not remembering the smallest detail of.

I had kept diaries or journals since my mid-twenties,

but like writing itself, I hadn't known just how to do it. I began by writing down everything—that is, if I wrote anything at all. Eventually I saw that I should not be saving trash.

I had written some short stories, but they were not any good. I didn't know how to go on with writing. The trouble with the stories was their lack of shape and their earnestness. I read stories in the *New Yorker* and *Esquire* and tried to imitate them. This imitation was a discouraging thing. My stories seemed like theirs, but somehow they could be distinguished from the genuine, or so I was convinced. Of course, in some cases they were just imitations of imitations, and no one is looking for that.

My problem was also belief even after I finished a novel. When I had finally decided to change course, to resign my commission and begin another life, it was a simple act physically: I wrote a letter of resignation and delivered it by hand. I thought there would be some reaction, someone would shake his head with regret at the departure of a regular officer with twelve years of service, but there was none. It was taken matter-of-factly, as if I were turning in a pair of boots. That afternoon I felt shaken and depressed. I wanted to talk to someone who would understand it. My former wing commander, whom I respected and who liked me, was at the time stationed in Washington, and I called him. He immediately invited me to dinner. I told him what I had just done and why, and what I hoped to do. He said, "You idiot."

I DIDN'T want to write in the city. In the city everyone was working or on their way to work, or it was afterwards and they had done their work for the day. And there was always the faint hum of the city like some huge generators buried deep underground that fell silent sometimes but not really. If you listened, in the silence they were always going.

I had two or three friends, artists, who also had unconventional lives, but they weren't married or had no children. Although one of them was married to Yoko Ono—this was long before John Lennon—and they did.

I tried to work in some borrowed places, but I couldn't bring any belief with me. I felt it was only possible at home, in the house early in the morning before my wife and two young daughters were awake or when they had gone to bed. I wrote in our bedroom on a long table. I was able to be at peace with myself then. In the daytime I worried about how I was going to earn a living. I had some money from the movie sale of my one novel, the novel that let me believe I could change my life, but that wouldn't last very long. I'd been a flying officer with experience, so I joined the air national guard. That paid a little.

The first story of mine that was published was about Barcelona. There are two German girls in the story, both of them unhappy. I would describe it further by saying that not a lot happens. One of the girls is based on someone I met at a *Fasching* ball. I don't remember her costume exactly, but it was like a bathing suit with gold scales and a skirt. Her friend—a man—in Barcelona was a literary person and also seemed something of a playboy. He knew everything about the city but disappeared after that first night. The next day we went to the beach. And that's it. That's the story, but the difference this time was that I was able to write it. It was the language, the assurance. I knew only a limited amount about the German girls, but I pressed down hard, so to speak. I somehow made it count.

I expected people to be impressed by the story. Most of them didn't understand the title, which was unnecessarily written in German, or know that it was also the title of a painting. It didn't occur to me that anyone might not be bothered to find that out— the authority of it would compel them to.

Is the story good? It's hard to know; it was then. Now it appeals to me because of its allusion to the whole nihilistic business of Tangier—Paul Bowles, Ginsberg, Burroughs, but especially Francis Bacon and his sadistic, drunken ex-RAF lover, Peter Lacy, and the moving landscape painting Bacon did there.

The writer is usually not the one to go to for an evaluation of his own work, in any case. I heard Joe Heller one evening ask a woman if she had read *Something Happened*, his lesser-known but significant novel. Yes, she'd read it. "Isn't that a wonderful book?" he said.

He was consistent. I overheard him in an interview with a French journalist during a writer's conference in Paris. After a few questions, the journalist said, "But, Monsieur Heller, after *Catch 22*, you never wrote anything that good again."

"Who has?" Heller said.

Writers are always judging other writers, but it's against their interests to closely evaluate themselves.

The writer is writing something. Because of a book's length and the various, even if slightly different, meanings of certain words, kinds of usage, the reader may actually be reading something else, even the reader it was intended for.

At bottom, writing is simple. It's fundamental, like a hammer and nails, or putting it another way, like singing a song. Or talking to yourself. It does have rules of order. It has grammar and syntax, the form and structure of sentences and the relationship and arrangement of words, most of which you learn even if incorrectly as a child by listening and imitating, repetition. Winston Churchill was a poor student. In preparatory school he was considered too stupid or stubborn to do Latin and Greek and was put instead into the English class with the other dullards who were considered unfit to learn anything more difficult. As he said,

> We were considered such dunces that we could learn only English . . . mere English. . . . Thus I got into my bones the essential structure of the ordinary British sentence—which is a noble thing. And when in years my schoolfellows who had won prizes and distinction for writing such beautiful Latin poetry . . . had to come down again to common English, to earn their living or earn their way, I did not feel myself at any disadvantage.

Making the shape and rhythm of sentences intensely felt was part of the teaching method at the writing school that James Jones and a woman named Lowney Handy established in Illinois in the years after the war. Jones was in the long process of writing his novel *From Here to Eternity,* and Lowney Handy was his muse. Students at the school sat for several

hours every day copying out by hand passages written by Hemingway, Faulkner, and Thomas Wolfe to
imbibe their strength and quality. It was the mimetic
method, perhaps not as ridiculous as it sounds.

I would say that teaching writing is more like
teaching dancing. If someone has a sense of rhythm,
you might teach them something. There's a great
longing in people to be able to write, and the teaching of it, fiction and poetry, has become widespread
in colleges and universities and outside of them as
well. The teachers are often well known and eagerly
sought. Some are virtual gurus with doctrines and
followers. In various cities there are private classes
with selected students. You hear of a dramatic figure
striking in appearance, wearing boots and jodhpurs,
perhaps, with long white hair like a prophet and bear-
ing a kind of literary ichor, the fluid in the veins of
the gods. He has a limitless number of great—known
and lesser-known—books and authors at his finger-
tips, just as a musician knows a thousand pieces. He
speaks only the truth, the core truth, about everything and the truth about you, as a writer and as a
person, which of necessity is likely to be hard. The
class sessions are long, lasting for hours, and cannot be interrupted. Questions are not permitted. In
this intensely charged atmosphere, the students read
their stories aloud, and he stops them when they have

made enough mistakes. For some that is after a few sentences. Others are allowed to go to the end. The importance of the first sentence, he insists, can't be overemphasized. It leads the way into the story. It sets its tone and also dictates the sentence that follows. Never begin a sentence with an adverb—it only tells what the sentence itself should reveal.

So, his passion, energy, and commitment are enormous. This is the boot camp method. You either drop out or become one of them. Somehow it goes against the idea of freedom of art. And yet, he reveals things to them. I never met one of his former students who wasn't loyal to, even loved him.

I THINK it was Turgenev or, if not, the de Goncourts who said that whenever men dine together, the talk is about women and love. Anyway, that was true of Saul Bellow, at least in the years that I knew him, the late 1970s and '80s. Women were especially on his mind at the time since his ex-wife—his third—was suing him for more money, given that he'd received the Nobel Prize with the six or seven hundred thousand dollars that came with it. The case was being tried in Chicago, and he was afraid the judge had been bribed. I never met his ex-wife, although I feel I know her. She was in the hands, so to speak, of a fabulous storyteller. Bellow was in the judge's hands and she was in Bellow's. She wanted increased alimony and child support. This was in Aspen, where he'd been invited for the summer by the Institute; as he swam, frog-like—there was a pool—he gave reasons why he suspected the judge and why it was obvious she had her eye on the prize money. More than her eye.

I loved hearing his stories about it. I was jealous of them—of the stories, that is. The rest of it seemed a terrible headache. It wasn't only his ex-wife, the beautiful archfeminist, it was a number of other women, some of whom I knew. What did I think of them? This one was rather nice, no? She had wanted to have an affair with him—I shouldn't have listened, he said.

I was younger, of course, though only by ten years, and I may have seemed freer and less troubled to him. We'd been driving in the mountains down toward Glenwood, beautiful rolling hayfields in the valley below. It would be wonderful to have a cabin up there, he said, away from everything but with a few friends around, where he could come and write. We could share a cabin. He'd be there a couple of months a year, he said, and I'd have it the rest of the time.

Getting away from women didn't make much sense since women were his means of ignition, but

we went ahead and bought some land and eventually
had a cabin there that neither of us used. It was not
long after this, however, that I began the first pages
of something he had suggested I write, which was
my memory of Virginia from the days when I first
knew my wife, and then after we were married. He
encouraged me to do it. I was a rookie and put a lot of
weight on what he said.

I had a novel that I was writing then. It was *Light
Years,* which I once described as being like the worn
stones of conjugal life: everything ordinary, everything marvelous, everything that makes it full or
makes it embittered—it goes on for years, decades,
and in the end seems to have passed like things seen
from a train, a meadow there, trees, houses, darkened
towns, a station going by. Everything not written
down disappears except for certain lasting moments,
certain people, days. The animals die, the house is
sold, the children are grown, even the couple themselves have vanished, and yet there is this poem.

I read it again about ten years ago. It's this musical
composition, interwoven, melancholy at times, posing
as a book. It's meant to be heroic, how one should use
the gift of life—I hate to say that, it sounds too good-
hearted. She was beautiful, but that's gone. He was
devoted but not able to take hold of life. The title was
originally *Nedra and Viri*—in my books the woman

is always stronger. If you can believe the book—and it's true—there was this dense world built on matrimony, a life enclosed, as it says, within time-honored walls. It's about the memory of those days.

I gave it to Saul to read, before it was published. He didn't quite see all that. He said a wonderful thing. He said it was really about the sexual heartlessness of women—their new role, and they were devastating in it.

Things you have written don't grow old with you, at least so it seems to me. It's true they may seem marked by time, but there's no such thing as being up to date when the time is past. They either go on outside of any date or cease to exist. Literature proceeds this way. Books mark a period or place, and then gradually they become that place and time.

BURNING the Days, which is an autobiography, was written only because of the encouragement of my editor, Joe Fox—I now think a mistaken encouragement. Why did he want me to write it? I obviously didn't want to. I didn't want to reveal all the personal things that were the underpinnings, psychological and factual, to whatever I might otherwise write. I didn't want to waste on a single book all the material—let's call it matter since much of it belonged to people other than me—that had accumulated in, say, fifty years. But several things made me start.

Rust Hills, at the time, was the fiction editor of *Esquire,* one of the two or three magazines that would print a story of mine. *Esquire* was respected and payment was prompt. Hill's list was headed by Richard Ford and DeLillo, two of his favorite writers, but he was a convivial man, and I had drinks with him from time to time. One day he called and asked me if I could come into town and have lunch with the editor in chief, who was named Lee Eisenberg and whom I'd never met.

At lunch it was explained to me that *Esquire,* with the aim of doing something new, was planning to eliminate the regular pages of text and illustrations or photographs and present a bolder look consisting of strong images and text that was not chopped up. There would be just four important blocks of writing that would, as they described it, anchor the issue and mark the decade. Their subject matter would be categories that were important to men, core issues. They wanted me to write one of them. Sport was already assigned.

Eisenberg said, "You're a man of the world. You've been married three or four times. We'd like you to write about sex and marriage."

I said there was some mistake. I hadn't been married three or four times. I'd only been married once, and didn't want to pose as expert as far as the other subject went.

After some silence I mentioned something that might be related to their idea. As a young man I had fallen deeply in love—this was in Honolulu when I'd been stationed there—with the wife of my closest friend. It would be about love and loyalty. Faithfulness. Ultimately the essay became "The Captain's Wife." And from that, over some years, came the book.

To write about oneself, selflessly, is difficult. It's not a matter of technique. I wasn't sure how far to take confession, to rip open the seams. At the same time, why would anyone be interested in my life unless it was written like a novel? To some extent the book was. It ends like this:

During the week before New Year I made some lists, jotted things, really: Pleasures, those that remained to me; Ten Closest Friends; Books Read. I also thought of various people as you do at year's end. Did Not Make the Voyage: my mother's baby sister who died, I think, named; George Cortada; Kelly; Joe Byron; Thomas Maynard, aged eight; Kay's miscarried child. . . .

Late in the day we walked on the deserted beach.

Afterwards I bathed, dressed, put on a white turtleneck, and, looking in the mirror, combed my hair. I had seen worse. Health, good. Hopes, fair.

Karyl Roosevelt and Dana, her son, came for drinks. She had been the most beautiful woman. Perhaps as a consequence her life had been devoted to men. Even afterwards she spoke of them with affection.

She'd been married to a very rich man. The first time they went to Europe they flew directly to Yugoslavia and boarded Marshal Tito's yacht. Tito, his sleeves rolled up, rowed her around a bay near Dubrovnik himself.

We drove to dinner at Billy's. Very few customers. Then back to the house before midnight, where we made a fire, drank toasts, and read aloud from favorite books. I read the last speech in Noël Coward's *Cavalcade,* the one in which the wife toasts her husband. They have lost both their sons in the war (1914–1918) and she drinks to them, to what they might have been, and to England. Kay read from *Ebenezer Le Page.* Karyl, the last part of Joyce's "The Dead," where the snow is falling on all Ireland, also from *Anna*

Karenina, Humboldt's Gift, and *The Wapshot Chronicle.* Dana read Robert Service, Stephen King, and Poe, something long and incomprehensible. Perhaps it was the drinks. "As the French say, *comment*?" Kay remarked.

The fire had burned to embers, the company was gone. We walked in the icy darkness with the old, limping dog. Nothing on the empty road, no cars, no sound, no lights. The year turning, cold stars above. My arm around her. Feeling of courage. Great desire to live on.

We lived on, not everyone. Dana was killed in an airplane crash fifteen years later. It was one of those planes made from fabricated parts that you assemble yourself. He had stopped by to say hello to us the day of the crash. He was a great-grandson of FDR.

I feel I should have written all this in another form. The novel was the god, and writers I knew were engaged with little else. John Updike was an exception. Apart from him, James Jones and William Styron were friends, and Styron and Mailer were until they had a serious fight about something that Mailer had heard Styron said about him or his wife. They, all of them, were always talking about the Great American Novel: Had it been written? Who was going to write it? They didn't count Melville or Faulkner. It was going to be one of them, and they were always working on it. Mailer talked about it most. I don't know if writers are talking about this great, mythic work anymore, or should I say at present. The attitude seems to be that the reign of the novel has ended, the traditional literary novel and its long-standing concerns of character and fate. Some veteran writers have said that it's over, Roth, Margaret Atwood, Doris Lessing. I'm not sure. I don't think that's the way it will be written anyway, by aiming at it. I think you have to be looking elsewhere. We will have greats, however—I think we can assume that—I mean in this century.

The writers I place highest are Nabokov, Faulkner, and Saul Bellow and Isaac Singer—I put the last two together because of qualities they share. I like Nabokov because of his ingenuity and verbal brilliance, his voice and style. I've said I believe those things last, the subjects aside. He was very witty. I talked with him for nearly an hour once in the bar of his hotel-residence in Montreux. It was in the winter—Montreux, not exactly a joyous place, seemed empty and the great old hotel did, too. There was no one else in the bar—Nabokov and Vera, his wife, in a blue Rodier suit. The dining room the night before had also been almost empty, with a number of waiters in white coats standing around motionless. In the bar, Nabokov was wary, commanding, polite. He made some funny remarks, but his wife sat impassive.

"You see?" he said. "She never laughs. She is married to the greatest clown in Europe, but she never laughs."

By chance, some years later, I met a man—I think a mathematician—who had shared an office with Nabokov at Cornell.

"What did you talk about?" I asked.

"Oh, he talked about things he'd read in the *National Enquirer*. He bought it every day. And he liked to talk about time."

"Time? What about time?"

"He'd hold up his wrist and say, 'I make it out to be 8:26. What do you have?'"

I FEEL a certain connection with Faulkner although I never met him or ever saw him. I know that he wanted to be a pilot and fly in the First World War, but he wasn't able to—he was rejected. He took up flying later and for a time owned an airplane, flying all over and participating in meets and even air races before finally giving it up.

I know one story about him and flying, not first-but secondhand through a man named Delmont Sylvester who was a pilot in the same wing with me. Sylvester was slightly effete and seemed to have been

somehow shamed though I never knew any reason
for it. Around 1952 he was stationed at an airfield
in Greenville, Mississippi, recalled to active duty
during the Korean War. He was the public relations
officer for the wing at Greenville, and a librarian in
town that he'd become friendly with offered to introduce him to Faulkner if he was interested. So he and
Faulkner met, Sylvester said. Faulkner was drunk
and had a bottle in his pocket. They talked about flying and the days when Faulkner had been a flyer in
France, which he hadn't been but it suited him to
remember it that way. The entire scenario of flyers in
the war reeked of glory. Faulkner had written poems
about it. He claimed he was a short story writer from
having failed as a poet, and a novelist, having failed
as a story writer. The idea of failure also showed up
when he was asked, as he was more than once, who
were the best American writers. He would say they
all had failed, but that Thomas Wolfe had been the
finest failure and William Faulkner the second finest.

That day in Greenville, Faulkner offered to write
a story about the air force in exchange for a ride in a
jet. There was a regulation that permitted civilians to
be given flights if it was in the interest of the air force,
and Sylvester promptly called the base commander,
who was a colonel, and explained the proposal. The

colonel listened to it all. At the end he said, "Who's Faulkner?"

FAULKNER and Nabokov both wrote movies, Nabokov just one. I wrote a dozen. That's as far as a connection goes.

Film. Movies. Writers all love movies, but there is a kind of nonrecognition of them on the part of literature. The Writers Guild is carefully divided into Writers Guild East and West, and in the American Academy of Arts and Letters there is architecture, music, art, and writing, including poetry, but no mention of film, which has been on the point of devouring it all. In any event, they have their own Academy.

One evening, going back to the time when I had written only a single book, I was taken by a friend to the house of an English director who at the end of dinner asked me if I would be interested in writing a film. I was very interested. The house was luxurious, just off Fifth Avenue. I knew nothing about film except as a member of the audience. Of course, that's not true; everyone knows something about it. The director gave me a book to read, a cheap paperback, he admitted, about a young model in Rome who might be a prostitute—for unknown reasons it had caught his interest. She turns out not to be, but the suspicion of it in the mind of her husband ruins their lives.

That was the beginning of a long period of finding work as a screenwriter, irregular for the most part. In between, I sold calendars and worked in a bookstore. The films were only occasionally made. The art of film turned out to be the art of raising money. On some films that could take years. It sometimes seemed that the less the amount needed, the harder it was to raise. Orson Welles was a figure of magnitude—he'd made *Citizen Kane* and much more. He had a long-held ambition to make a movie about Falstaff. Welles's body and voice were majestic, and he was eminently suited for the role, one of the most memorable in English drama.

He never could raise the money. It was late in his career, and he was considered unreliable, his artistic temperament had cost too many people too much. He therefore began shooting pieces of the movie whenever he could, disbanding the small crew and then trying to assemble them again when he could afford to shoot more. It was disheartening. It was a struggle. His Italian wife had given him all the encouragement she could. "Orson," she said at last, "if they took all the film in the world and put it in a room and burned it, what difference would it make?"

If it was not money, it was chasing after actors and actresses, waiting to hear something. At the time, European films had risen to heights of prestige and were looked upon with envy. The innovative French and Italian directors who had written their own scripts were called *auteurs,* authors of the movie. Godard was like a rock star. People in Paris could take you to the street that Belmondo died on in *Breathless.* Truffaut and Fellini were revered. I was intoxicated, too. It was easy to be disheartened by what the culture admired, but here it seemed right. Roberto Rosselini, rotund and balding, had married Ingrid Bergman—effectively, that is. She had left her surgeon husband and two children and had had two daughters with Rosselini. Nothing rivaled the new adulation. Antonioni—Michelangelo Antonioni—was shooting his 1966 movie *Blow-Up,* with Peter Bowles. When Bowles questioned a directorial choice, Antonioni put his arms around Bowles, pulled him close, and said, "Peter, believe in me. Trust me. I am not God, but I am Michelangelo Antonioni."

This wasn't Hollywood and the big, gated studios, the factories. In Europe it was happening on the street, so to speak. I went to London to meet Polanski—to be looked over by him, rather. He struck me as being someone essentially without sentiment. Nevertheless, I was hired. The movie that came from that, *Downhill Racer,* was actually made, though by that time Polanski had nothing to do with it. He called me Jimmy. Elsa Martinelli called me Jeemy. There was an ambience to all of it, hectic, passionate, and a little cheap. Anything was liable to be compromised. I don't think that that many people set out to make something beautiful, but then nobody sets out to make a bad movie.

It was during this time and due to these involvements that I met Ben Sonnenberg, a bibliophile who, in the course of spending all he could of his inheritance, founded the literary magazine *Grand Street* in which he published some of my stories, "the ones you didn't give to *Esquire,*" he complained.

I was to meet him on Division Street in a restaurant. It was dark. The banks were closed. Chinese people were getting out of cars. A youngish man was sitting at a table with some books and four bottles of Japanese beer.

"Do you know Chinese cooking?" he asked me. He had a clear, soft voice with a faint English tone.

I said, no.

"Then permit me to order for you," he said.

He had quit school before finishing high school, he told me, in order to live his own life. He had never gone to college. He went to London instead, for polish and to buy books and clothes.

There was some sort of rubbery peeling in the soup. I asked him what it was.

"Yes, it's something I wondered about myself," he said. "Fish tripe."

He had a life of reading and going to the theater. He also translated plays, forgotten French and Belgian boulevard plays. I had to believe it was just another perversity. He liked to talk about movies and what my percentage of profits was, pretending I had one. Didn't I find that dramatic writing weakened the power to write fiction, however? It was so much more concise, and it had no description, none at all. In addition, it was relentlessly dramatic, he said, which was not the way of patient, revealing writing.

He was making me feel uneasy, but I later was grateful for it.

I didn't tell him about the novel I had just made some first notes for. The title, *Toda*, came from Victor Hugo's coded symbols in his notebooks concealing his many sexual activities from Juliette Drouet, his longtime mistress. Along with a woman's name or initials, he might mark an *N* that stood for naked; something else for caresses; *Suisses*, for breasts; and so forth, a kind of ascending order. For everything, the full act, he wrote *toda*, all. There was something noted for almost every day.

At another Chinese restaurant down the street he handed me the books to hold while he went in to use the restroom. I stood in the doorway—a book of Elizabethan drama, a novel by V. S. Naipaul, the *Sunday Observer*. I read a few pages of the Naipaul, five extraordinary pages.

Why, I thought, was I living so far from the people who interested me?

Sonnenberg not long afterwards became ill, in fact I was witness to it. I noticed him scuff his toe going in a doorway. He was having some slight trouble walking, and the next time I saw him he had a very elegant cane. He was only about thirty-five and had been diagnosed with multiple sclerosis. It eventually left him paralyzed from the neck down. He could no longer even turn the page of a book. His wife read to him, and friends came to read. He continued to edit *Grand Street* until the money ran out, at which point he sold it. He never lost his taste for fine things or his memory of them although the words "fine things" would make him wince.

I BEGAN to write *Toda* when an inspired description of what the novel would be came to me late one night as I was sitting very tired in a darkened room in a hotel just above Gramercy Park. I went into the bathroom, turned on the light, and quickly wrote it down. It was a page long. I knew that great fortune had struck me. What I had written, the issues of the book, were so clear. The thing is, I lost that piece of paper—I simply could never find it again—although it didn't make that much difference since I'd in the meantime changed my mind about the central figure, who it should be.

I write much the way everyone does, I think. I try to write regularly. I have difficulty beginning each day. If I can leave myself a line or a few words to help me take it up again, it goes a little better. The day sometimes goes well. More often it doesn't. I'm reconciled to the certainty that I'll be disappointed in what I've written. I write when I don't feel like it, but not when it revulses me. I think I write for a certain kind of person—I'm not going to define exactly who, probably a woman—but not for everybody. An intelligent woman, as Babel said.

I write by hand with a pen. Then I type it on an electric typewriter. I could just as easily use a laptop but I like the sound, slightly irregular, of the keys hitting. I type with two fingers.

I'm actually composing, in a sense. I'm listening to the words as I write them, to groups of words. I like to go again and again over their sound to lead me on to the next sentences. Sometimes I write down a little on what I intend to write, a few words to show the way, and that I may even want to include, but it's all depending.

The main thing is organization—finding order. There are so many things—too many—to hold in your head about a novel or even a chapter. There can't be confusion. For *Toda* I drew a chronological line to begin—it was that kind of book—and marked everything along that line. I had pushpins in a big board, one or two for each chapter, and the odd notes and details for the chapter, I pinned there.

You don't do all the writing at your desk. You do it elsewhere, carrying the book with you. The book is your companion, you have it in your mind all the time, running through it, alert for links to it. It becomes your chief companion, in the real sense of the word, you can talk to it quietly. It becomes your sole companion.

The writing may go on for ten days, as with George Simenon, or weeks, or months, or years. It's the same thing for everyone.

I made two thick notebooks for this book, reference books divided into sections holding things from my journals that might be of some use: weather, places, conversation, faces, deaths, love, sex, people. *Toda.* I didn't use even a quarter of it.

I worked on the book for a year, perhaps more, and then lost confidence in it. It was a question of the wrong principal character. After a while I began again, but when you change a central thing it necessarily changes other things.

I mentioned earlier the freedom of art. I mean by that the freedom not to be bound by common ideas of morality or by any catechism. I mean also the freedom—really the need—to break through any mediating things. There should be no prohibitions to what you are allowed to think or imagine.

The language, English, which we kick around—it has no guardians—is nevertheless an important, almost a sacred thing. It bears everything along on it and by it. So I try and pay attention to that.

In the end they said, you can't call the book *Toda*. Nobody knows what that means. I argued with them, but the publisher said, no, you have to have a different title. So I called it *All That Is*.

I'll just read the epigraph:

There comes a time when you realize that everything is a dream, and only those things preserved in writing have any possibility of being real.